Electric Pressure Cooker Cookbook Box Set

160 Electric Pressure Cooker Recipes For Breakfast, Brunch, Appetizers, Desserts, Dinner, Soups And Stews

3 Books In 1

D1552456

ROSA BARNES

ISBN-13: 978-1514301524

ISBN-10: 1514301520

DEDICATION

To all who desire to put good food on the table without getting stuck all day in the kitchen.

TABLE OF CONTENTS

BOOK 1

Electric Pressure Cooker Cookbook

Vol.1 55 Electric Pressure Cooker Dinner Recipes

ROSA BARNES

INTRODUCTION

The pressure cooker is one of the most wondrous kitchen tools ever invented. Cooking has never been this fast, easy and simple with this gadget. And I bet you also have been giving this cooker a well deserved thank you for making life a bit easier.

From the time I learned how to work around the kitchen, the electric pressure cooker has become my frequent companion. From simple beef soup to the more complex ones, cooking with it has always been a breeze. Here are some advantages of having one:

1. Cooking time is shortened, obviously. It is much faster to cook in a pressure cooker, hence it is time-saving. The toughest meat is turned tender and succulent in a much faster way than the conventional cooking method.

2. Food nutrients are much more intact than in conventional cooking because of reduced liquid usage. Meat and vegetables retain much of their nutritional value because cooking is done in a virtually airtight container.

3. Kitchen mess is minimized because food is cooked in a sealed container such that splashes or blots are not a problem.

4. For me, food tastes better, if not best. The sealed cooking method locks in flavor and helps infuse seasoning to the food while cooking.

If you have just bought a pressure cooker, well, let me congratulate you for investing in this very helpful gadget. And while you may be so excited to try it out, you might as well have to learn the basics, as this will be of great help in getting the best out of your pressure cooker.

GETTING FAMILIAR WITH YOUR ELECTRIC PRESSURE COOKER

Most, if not all, pressure cookers come with an instruction manual. Take extra time to read it and familiarize yourself. Additionally, here is some information for you:

1. Inside most pressure cookers you will find a mark for maximum fill. As the term implies, don't overfill your pressure cooker above this mark.

2. Pressure cooking generally uses less liquid than with the usual method of cooking. In contrast, it also requires adequate amount of liquid to create steam, for each 15-minute extra cooking time, additional 1 cup of liquid is needed.

3. To achieve full flavor when cooking meat, better fry them until all sides are brown. Additionally, lessen the amount of seasonings, including salt. This is to avoid concentration of flavors that usually happens when pressure cooking.

4. Familiarize yourself with the cooking time for different ingredients needed for your dish, to avoid under- or overcooking. Of course, you would not want your finished product to be all mushy, right?

5. When the pressure cooker has reached its full or maximum pressure, that's the time you count for the cooking time.

RELEASING THE PRESSURE

The pressure from your cooker may be released in two ways:

1.The natural or slow release method, where you just remove the cooker from heat, and just wait for the pressure to come out naturally in 10 to 15 minutes.

This is usually done in meat soups and stews, beans, pasta, and cereals. This method also gives additional "softening time" for the food as heat is still inside the cooker for a long time, although released gradually.

2. The quick release method, which is perfect for fish, vegetables and poultry, where you put your cooker into the sink, and pour cold water on top of it until the pressure is released. For other models of pressure cookers, check if they come with an automatic release method. This method works best for vegetables so as to avoid over-cooking.

SAFETY TIPS

Your electric pressure cooker is a helpful kitchen companion and its efficiency will be maximized so long as you follow its correct usage. Many stories have been said about its misuse, however most pressure cookers nowadays have added extra safety measures to assure users that we are not jeopardizing our safety.

1. Check for the rubber ring of your cooker, if it is still flexible and in good working condition to ensure that pressure is still sealed when cooking.

2. Check all valves for food particles or any dirt that may block the passage of pressure. Simply put, make sure the valves are clean.

3. Do not use oil or fat as the only liquid for pressure cooking. It won't create enough steam! Best use water, soup stock, wine, or milk.

4. Always refer to the instruction manual of your pressure cooker. Different models have different features. In general, when the cooker reaches its maximum heat, it produces a loud hissing sound. If that happens, lower or reduce the heat source.

5. Do not overfill the cooker because it might result in clogging up of food in the valves.

6. Make sure that the cooker has enough liquid for pressure build-up.

7. When in use, never leave the pressure cooker unattended for a long period of time.

Lastly, the collection in this book are my well-loved recipes which are tried and tested at home and with family and friends, grouped and selected to give you the best no more, no less. I consider these recipes as the best 'versions'. With this collection, you have the freedom to cook according to your tastes and make use of ingredients that are readily available. In addition, you can mix and match to create dishes that are uniquely of your own style, with the flavors that you call your own.

Enjoy and have fun cooking!

Rosa Barnes

PORK RECIPES

Easy Creamy Pork Chops

Would you like to try this creamy and perfect-to-the-bite pork chops? Its texture and taste will definitely make you want more of this recipe. Easy to prepare, it's perfect for you who want to have a nice meal anytime of the day without having to sacrifice time.

Preparation Time: 10 minutes

Cooking Time: 10 minutes

Number of Servings: 4

Ingredients:

Pork chops, 4 slices

Olive oil, 2 tablespoons

Chicken powder or bouillon, 2 teaspoons

Cream of mushroom soup, 1 can

Water, 1 cup water

Sour cream, 1 cup sour cream

Pepper, for seasoning

Parsley, snipped

Cooking Instructions:

1. Lightly season pork chops with pepper.

2. Meanwhile, put olive oil in the pressure cooker, bring to medium heat.

3. Fry pork chops until both sides are brown. Set aside on a platter.

4. In the pressure cooker, pour water and add chicken powder. Mix until dissolved. Make sure that the bottom of the cooker is scraped and completely deglazed.

5. Place the browned pork chops into the cooker, cover and cook for about 8 minutes in high pressure.

6. Remove from heat and release steam carefully. Open cooker and remove pork chops. Set aside.

7. Put back cooker on medium heat, add mushroom soup. Bring to a boil and stir constantly for two minutes. Remove from heat.

8. Arrange the pork chops in a platter. Pour in the sour cream and mushroom soup, and top with parsley. Enjoy!

Spanish-Style Braised Pork

This simple, easy-to-prepare recipe captures the long-time tradition of Spain in terms of braising pork. Rich and flavorful, this pork dish combines spices and flavors that you can adjust depending to your taste. So come and let's try this, amigos!

Preparation Time: 10 minutes

Cooking Time: 75 minutes

Number of Servings: 6 to 8

Ingredients:

Pork butt, 4.5 lb

Olive oil, 2 tablespoons

Onion, minced, ¼ cup

Garlic powder, ¼ cup

Paprika, 1 tablespoon

Chicken stock, 2 cups

Red wine, 2 cups

Lemon juice, 1/2 cup

Mushrooms, sliced (optional)

Pearl onions, sliced (optional)

Cooking Instructions:

1. In a bowl, properly mix the first five ingredients together. Transfer the mixture into the pressure cooker.

2. Top the mixture with chicken stock, lemon juice, and red wine.

3. Ensure that the pressure cooker will not be overfilled, meaning there should be enough space left between the ceiling of the cooker cover and the meat surface.

4. Heat the pressure cooker to high. After reaching the maximum heat possible, maintain it by turning down heat. Cook for a maximum of 45 minutes.

5. Turn off heat, let cool for 15 minutes. Release pressure from the cooker.

6. Transfer contents of the cooker into a serving dish. Embellish with mushrooms and pearl onions, if desired. Serve hot.

Additional notes:

1. The ingredients may be adjusted according to the capacity of your cooker.

2. You may try other pork cuts, like pork loin. Accordingly cooking time may be adjusted.

3. Try adding veggies on your dish, such as baby carrots, broccoli, or potatoes as garnishing.

Chinese Char Siu

Char siu is a Chinese dish that is exquisitely flavored and somewhat exotic. This recipe has a different style of cooking, it utilizes the good old reliable pressure cooker, instead of traditional grilling.

This dish is best served with green veggies, with rice, and with barbeque sauce.

Preparation Time: 15 minutes

Cooking Time: 50 minutes

Number of Servings: 6

Ingredients:

Pork belly, trimmed, 2 lb

Soy sauce, 4 tablespoons

Chicken stock, 4 cups

Char siu sauce, 8 tablespoons (found at Asian food stores)

Dry sherry, 2 tablespoons

Sesame oil, 2 teaspoons

Honey, 2 tablespoons

Peanut oil, 1 teaspoon

Cooking Instructions:

1. Mix the chicken stock, soy sauce, sherry, and four tablespoons of char siu sauce in the uncovered pressure cooker. Cook in medium heat for five to eight minutes.

2. Add pork belly, cover the pressure cooker, allow pressure to build up, and cook for 30 minutes more. Turn off heat and allow to cool naturally.

3. Transfer pork to a platter and let cool. Chop into thin medium sized cuts. Set aside any leftover cooking fluid in the cooker.

4. Prepare the coating mix in a bowl by stirring in the remaining char siu sauce, honey, and sesame oil.

5. Heat peanut oil and fry the pork on medium-high temperature. Brush pork with coating mix while frying, until it turns brown.

6. Simmer the leftover cooking fluid over medium-high temperature for three minutes.

7. Pour over arranged pork slices. Your dish is now ready to eat!

Pressure Cooker Roasted Pork Loin

For those who love the aroma and essence of garlic, tasting this dish one time would never be enough! Here's to the ever reliable pressure cooker, which makes things easy in the kitchen, while providing us with tasty, delectable and flavorful pork loin.

Preparation Time: 15 minutes

Cooking Time: 45 minutes

Number of Servings: 4

Ingredients:

Boneless pork loin, 2 lb

Water, 1cup

Carrots, 3 medium-sized, sliced

Onion, 1 medium-sized, quartered

Celery, 2 stalks, sliced

Potatoes, 3 medium-sized, quartered

Garlic, 6 cloves

Vegetable oil, 2 tablespoons

Bay leaf, 1 piece

Salt and pepper to taste

Cooking Instructions:

1. Using a knife, make small cuts on the pork loin, about 1 inch deep. Insert a clove of garlic in every hole, Sprinkle pork with salt and pepper.

2. In the uncovered pressure cooker, fry the pork in vegetable oil until all sides are brown.

3. Remove meat from the cooker and drain excess oil.

4. After the cooker has cooled down, add water, bay leaf and pork. Close the pressure cooker's lid and cook for 30 minutes.

5. After the time set, cool the pressure cooker and remove the meat.

6. Arrange the vegetables into the cooker and return the meat on top of the veggies.

7. Close the cooker's lid and cook for another 5 minutes. After cooking, let cool and release the pressure from the cooker. Remove the meat and vegetables.

8. Let cool for five minutes before carving and serving.

Boneless Pork Roast With Fennel Delight

Meat lovers will surely enjoy this mouth-watering dish! And with the help of the pressure cooker, this can easily be prepared any time of the day.

Preparation Time: 20 minutes

Cooking Time: 1 hour and 20 minutes

Number of Servings: 4

Ingredients:

Pork, boneless, 2 lb

White wine, 1/2 cup

Chicken stock, 1/2 cup

Garlic, peeled and crushed, 2 cloves

Olive oil, 2 tablespoons

Salt and pepper to taste

Onion, medium sized, sliced

Fennel bulbs, thickly sliced, 1 pound

Cooking Instructions:

1. Heat olive oil in the pressure cooker, add pork and season with salt and pepper. Brown all sides of the pork.

2. Remove pork from pot and transfer to a platter. Set aside.

3. In the same pressure cooker, Sauté garlic in the olive oil, add chicken stock and white wine. Bring to a boil then simmer.

4. Put back the pork into the cooker, close the lid and cook under pressure for 35 to 40 minutes.

5. Remove pressure from the cooker, open the lid and add the fennel and the onions. Close back the lid again and cook for 15 more minutes.

8. Take out the pork and vegetables from cooker, set aside but keep warm in a separate dish.

9. Continue to simmer the sauce left in the cooker, stirring constantly. If you want thicker sauce, add a tablespoon of flour. Mix well. Remove from fire and pour over the pork and vegetables.

10. Serve and enjoy!

Pressure Cooked Pulled Pork

My ever-versatile pulled pork provides dish variations. It can be served as a dish for dinner or lunch, for sandwiches, salads, and side dish for veggies. What is interesting is that when cooked in a pressure cooker, it doesn't lose its moisture and flavor. All you get is tender and tasty pork, delicioso!

Preparation Time: 10 minutes

Cooking Time: 80 minutes

Number of Servings: 6 to 8

Ingredients:

For the pulled pork:

Pork shoulder, cut in half, 3.5 lb

Water, 1 cup

Beer, 1 1/2 cup

Sugar, 6 tablespoons

Dry mustard, 2 teaspoons

Smoked paprika, 2 teaspoons

Salt, 1 teaspoon

For the sauce:

Apple cider vinegar, 1½ cup

Hot water, 1/2 cup

Black pepper, 1 teaspoon

Cayenne pepper, 1 teaspoon

Brown sugar, 2 tablespoons

Dry mustard, 2 teaspoons

Salt, 1 teaspoon

Cooking Instructions:

1. In a bowl, mix together sugar, paprika, dry mustard and salt. Use this mixture to rub over pork shoulder halves.

2. In the pressure cooker, mix beer and water. Add in the pork shoulder halves. Cover and lock the lid of the cooler, bring to high temperature for 75 to 80 minutes.

3. Turn off heat, remove pressure using quick release method. Uncover.

4. Separate the pork from the mixture and shred using two forks. All excess fat should be discarded.

5. Retain ½ only of the cooking juices in the pressure cooker. Discard the other half.

6. In a separate bowl, pour hot water and dissolve brown sugar by stirring thoroughly, Add in apple cider vinegar, salt, cayenne pepper, black pepper, and dry mustard. Mix thoroughly.

7. In the pressure cooker, add the shredded pork with the remaining cooking juices. Additionally, pour the apple cider vinegar sauce in the mixture.

8. Close the lid of the pressure cooker and bring to maximum heat for 2 to 3 minutes.

9. Remove from heat, release pressure using quick release method. Uncover.

10. When serving, use additional barbeque sauce depending on your taste.

Traditional Meaty Loaf

Who doesn't like meat loaf? It's basically everyone's favorite dish, young and old alike. Served with ketchup and enhanced with tomato sauce, pairing it with cubed potatoes will be heavenly.

Preparation Time: 10 minutes

Cooking Time: 40 minutes

Number of Servings: 4

Ingredients:

Beef, pork and veal, 1.5 lb mixed

Egg, 1 piece

Garlic, 1 clove

Salt, 1 teaspoon

Bread, 2 slices, soaked in water and squeezed dry

Pepper, freshly ground

Onion, 1 medium sized, minced

Parsley, 2 tablespoons

Chicken stock, 2 tablespoons

Olive oil, 2 tablespoons

Tomato sauce, 1 cup

Worcestershire sauce, 2 teaspoons

Water, 1 cup

Cooking instructions:

1. In a bowl, mix thoroughly the following ingredients: meat, salt, bread, onion, pepper, garlic, egg, Worcestershire sauce and chicken stock. From the mixture, shape into two small loaves. After wrapping each loaf in wax paper, chill for several hours until firm.

2. Heat olive oil in the pressure cooker. Fry the pork loaves until brown on all sides. Place in cooker basket. Remove excess oil from the cooker. In its place, mix water and tomato sauce, and season with pepper and salt.

3. Cover all sides of the meat loaves with ketchup and place in the pressure cooker while inside the cooker basket.

4. Cover the lid and cook the meat loaves under pressure for 15 minutes, after which remove the pressure through the quick release method. Remove from the cooker, slice and serve.

Missy's Pork Tenderloin

This marinated Pork tenderloin complements pasta, rice or potatoes. It's so easy to prepare, but also fantastically delicious. This is something that you should definitely try.

Preparation Time: 15 minutes, extra 8 hours for marinating

Cooking Time: 25 minutes

Number of Servings: 4

Ingredients:

Pork tenderloin, 1 lb

Chicken stock, 3/4 cup

Lemon juice, 4 tablespoons

Salt, ¼ teaspoon

Olive oil, 4 tablespoons

Lime juice, 4 tablespoons

Fresh coriander leaves, 4 tablespoons

Garlic, 2 cloves, sliced

Chilies, ½ teaspoon, crushed

Cooking Instructions:

1.In a juicer/smoothie maker, mix coriander, crushed chilies, olive oil, garlic, lime juice, and salt until smooth. Transfer to a large resealable plastic bag. Put the pork tenderloins into the bag, seal and massage well. Make sure that air has been removed from the bag before sealing. Marinate for 8 hours or overnight.

2.In the pressure cooker, mix together the chicken stock and lemon juice. Arrange the pork tenderloins into the liquid mixture. Add the remaining marinade from the bag into the cooker.

3.Close the lid of the cooker and cook over high temperature until it whistles. Reduce to medium and simmer for 25 minutes. Remove from heat and let cool. Remove pressure and open the lid. Slice the pork tenderloins before serving.

Shredded Pork And Barbeque Sauce

Quick, simple and delectable – these sum up this dish. Deliciously served as a main dish or as a sandwich filling. You can never get enough of this. And your kids would definitely love it too!

Preparation Time: 5 minutes

Cooking Time: 60 minutes

Number of Servings: 16

Ingredients:

Pork shoulder, 8 lb

Garlic granules, 1 teaspoon

Salt and pepper for seasoning

Barbeque sauce, 3 cups

Cooking Instructions:

1.Prepare pork for cooking by seasoning it with garlic granules, pepper and salt. Put in the pressure cooker and add water just enough to cover the pork.

2.Close the lid, cook in high temperature for one hour.

3.Remove from heat, and release pressure. Open the lid, discard the juice but set aside about 2 cups.

4.Shred the pork, place in a separate bowl, and mix with barbeque sauce. Add the reserved liquid according to your desired consistency.

Delightful Chili Pork

The juiciness and tenderness of this dish is something to look forward to. So delectable and yummy, the mix of pork, with peppers and chilies makes your mealtime satisfying. Try it now.

Preparation Time: 25 minutes

Cooking Time: 1 hour

Number of servings: 12

Ingredients:

Pork shoulder, 3 lb, boneless, cut into chunks

Fresh peppers, 2 medium sized, chopped

Chilies, 4 medium sized, chopped

Rapeseed oil, 3 tablespoons

Onion, 1 large size, chopped

Coriander, 2 teaspoons, ground

Garlic, 4 cloves, chopped

Cumin, 3 teaspoons, grounded

Beef stock, 1 ½ cup

Cooking Instructions:

1.Put oil in the pressure cooker, and bring to medium-high temperature. Cook pork until brown.

2.Add the rest of the ingredients to the pork.

3.Close lid of pressure cooker. Cook for 1 hour under medium steady pressure. Remove from heat and carefully release the pressure. Open the lid. Transfer contents to a serving bowl and serve. Easy does it!

Aloha Hawaiian Pork

Dazzle your taste buds with this delicious and delectable pork recipe filled with pineapple-flavored goodness.

Preparation Time: 15 minutes

Cooking Time: 15 minutes

Number of servings: 6 - 8

Ingredients:

Pork, 2 ½ lb, cut in 1" cubes

Onion, 1 medium size, sliced

Pineapple juice, 1 ½ cups

Oil, 4 tablespoons

Water, ½ cup

Brown sugar, ½ cup

Vinegar, ½ cup

Pineapple chunks, 2 cans (1 lb 4 oz each)

Green bell pepper, 1 cup, diced

Salt, 1 ½ teaspoon

Water, ½ cup

Cornstarch, 5 tablespoons

Soy sauce, 2 tablespoons

Cooking Instructions:

1.Heat oil in the pressure cooker. Fry pork and onion slices until brown.

2.Add water, pineapple juice, brown sugar, vinegar and salt. Close lid and bring to high temperature. Cook for 12 minutes.

3. Remove from heat and release pressure quickly. Open the lid, add pineapple chunks, green bell pepper and soy sauce.

4.In a separate bowl, mix cornstarch and water. Pour into the cooker, and stir constantly until sauce thickens.

5. Serve this dish over rice.

CHICKEN RECIPES

Pressure Cooked Lemony Chicken

Perfectly blended chicken and lemon brings lots of enjoyment to your dining table.

Preparation Time: 10 minutes

Cooking Time: 40 minutes plus 8 hours marinating time

Number of Servings: 4

Ingredients:

Chicken, cut in serving sizes, 3½ pounds

Lemon juice, ¼ cup

Chicken stock, ½ cup

Olive oil, ¼ cup and 2 tablespoons

Oregano, 2 teaspoons

Pepper and salt to taste

Cooking Instructions:

1. Combine together ¼ cup oil, oregano, lemon juice, pepper and salt. Marinate the chicken in the mixture overnight.

2. Remove from marinade and dry the chicken on paper towels. Season with salt and pepper. Don't forget to reserve the marinade.

3. Heat 2 tablespoons of oil in the pressure cooker. Fry the chicken until brown on all sides. Transfer chicken into a platter. Set aside.

4. Remove the oil from the pressure cooker. Replace with the reserved marinade and the chicken stock.

5. Close the lid of the cooker, heat to high pressure, then lower the heat and cook for 5 minutes. Remove from fire and release the pressure. Pour over the chicken. Serve and enjoy!

Rich Boneless Chicken

Richly-flavored and impressively delectable, this recipe usually takes one hour of cooking over ordinary cooking stoves, but with a pressure cooker, simmering takes only nine minutes.

Preparation Time: 10 minutes

Cooking Time: 9 minutes

Number of Servings: 4

Ingredients:

Chicken breast, 1 lb, boneless, cut into 2" cubes

Chicken stock, ¼ cup

Canola oil, 3 tablespoons

Sliced mushrooms, 14 ounces

White cooking wine, 1 cup

Onion, one medium sized, minced

Garlic powder, 2 teaspoons

Tomato paste, small can, 5.5 oz

Fresh basil, 1 small bunch

Thyme, ½ teaspoon

Cooking Instructions:

1.Brown chicken breast for 5 minutes, using canola oil in a pressure cooker.

2.After more or less five minutes, add the rest of the ingredients into the pressure cooker. Close the lid, lock and bring to very high pressure. Cook for 9 minutes.

3. Remove from heat and allow pressure to be released before removing the lid.

4. Use as a side dish with pasta.

Chicken In A Duck Sauce

This chicken dish is tasty and a nice addition to rice and broccoli. The duck sauce makes it all the more enticing to the palate.

Preparation Time: 10 minutes

Cooking Time: 9 minutes

Number of Servings: 4

Ingredients:

Olive oil, 1 tablespoon

Chicken, 3 lbs, cut in serving sizes

Salt and pepper

Paprika, ½ teaspoon

Marjoram, ½ teaspoon

Duck sauce, ½ cup

White wine, ¼ cup

Chicken stock, ¼ cup

Cooking Instructions:

1.In an open pressure cooker, brown chicken in olive oil.

2.Remove chicken from heat, transfer on a warm platter and mix with salt, paprika, pepper and marjoram.

3. Remove excess oil from the cooker, replace with wine and chicken stock. Place chicken on top of the mixture. Add duck sauce by brushing it on the chicken.

4. Close the lid and bring to high heat. As soon as it reaches its maximum temperature, lower the heat and cook for 8 minutes.

5. Remove pressure and open the lid. Get the chicken from the cooker and arrange in a platter. Boil the remaining liquid until thick. Spoon over the chicken and serve.

Casserole Chicken Dish

This is a very simple chicken dish that is truly everybody's favorite.

Preparation Time: 10 minutes

Cooking Time: 20 minutes

Number of Servings: 4

Ingredients:

Chicken, 3 lbs, cut in serving portions

Bacon, 2 slices, cut in 1" pieces

Potatoes, 3 medium sizes

Mushrooms, ¼ lb, fresh

Salt to taste

Pearl onions, 12 small pieces, peeled

Flour, 1 teaspoon

Brandy, 1 tablespoon

Chicken stock, ¼ cup

White wine, ¼ cup

Truffle pieces for garnish (optional)

Cooking Instructions:

1.Rub the chicken pieces with some salt. Set aside.

2.After peeling the potatoes, form them into small balls using a melon scoop. Set aside.

3.Heat the uncovered pressure cooker and sauté in it the bacon slices until the fat comes out. Remove the bacon from the pressure cooker. Set aside.

4.Fry potatoes until lightly golden using bacon fat. Once done, remove from cooker. Replace with the chicken pieces and fry until brown, too. Remove from the cooker and set aside.

5.Sauté mushrooms and onions for a minute using bacon fat. Add flour, brandy, wine and stock. Mix.

6.Add the bacon, chicken, and potatoes to the pressure cooker.

7. Close the lid. Heat and bring the cooker to high pressure. Cook for 8 minutes on high pressure.

8. After cooking, release the pressure and remove the lid. Transfer into a platter, and garnish with truffle pieces.

Mandarin-Infused Chicken

This recipe is of Chinese origin and delights everyone. With the tangy taste of mandarin oranges, it would definitely be a hit for chicken lovers everyone.

Preparation Time: 10 minutes

Cooking Time: 15 minutes

Number of Servings: 4

Ingredients:

Chicken breasts, ¾ lb, boneless and skinless

Chicken broth or stock, 2 cups

Balsamic vinegar, 1 tablespoon

Mandarin oranges, 1 can (11 oz), drained

Onion, 1 piece, sliced thinly

Tarragon, 1 teaspoon, dried

Water, ¼ cup

Chinese wheat noodles, 8 ounces

Honey, 1 tablespoon

Soy sauce, 1 tablespoon

Cornstarch, 4 tablespoons

Pepper to taste, freshly ground

Cooking Instructions:

1.Combine chicken, onions, broth and vinegar in the pressure cooker. Close the lid, bring the pressure to high temperature, and cook for 5 minutes on high pressure.

2.Release pressure using the natural method then open the lid.

3.Transfer the chicken into a platter. Stir into the chicken stock mixture the oranges, honey, soy sauce and tarragon. In a separate bowl, dissolve cornstarch in water and pour into the stock mixture. Cook uncovered in moderate heat until thick.

4. Arrange cooked noodles in a platter, top with chicken and sauce. For final touches, add pepper to taste.

Mouthwatering Ginger Chicken

I absolutely adore this delectable recipe. Ginger adds that special flavor to chicken, making it so yummy you would want to eat more!

Preparation Time: 10 minutes

Cooking Time: 15 minutes

Number of Servings: 4

Ingredients:

Chicken, 3 lbs, cut into serving pieces

Canola oil, 3 tablespoons

Onion, 1 piece, sliced thinly

Ginger, 1 large piece, grated

Water, ¼ cup

Soy sauce, ¼ cup

Dry sherry, ¼ cup

Salt and pepper to taste

Cooking Instructions:

1.In an uncovered pressure cooker, brown chicken in canola oil. Remove chicken and replace with onions. Sauté until golden brown.

2.In another bowl, put chicken, ginger, sherry soy sauce and water. Mix well and transfer to the pressure cooker.

3. Close the lid and bring cooker to high temperature. When the maximum pressure is attained, lower heat and cook for 8 minutes. Remove from heat.

4. Release pressure either by quick or automatic method. Remove the lid and season chicken with salt and pepper.

5. Serve and enjoy!

Zesty Chicken With Pasta

We all long for something different, something that excites our taste buds just like this delicious recipe. Savor the spice and love the taste of chicken. So tempting.

Preparation Time: 30 minutes

Cooking Time: 15 minutes

Number of Servings: 4

Ingredients:

Chicken breasts, 1 lb, boneless and skinless

Chicken broth or stock, 1 cup

Scallions, 1 ½ cups

Garlic cloves, 4, minced

Ginger, 1 tablespoon, minced

Sweet red pepper, 1 small piece, cut into thin strips

Red pepper flakes, ½ teaspoon, crushed

Parsley, 2 tablespoons, chopped

Peanuts, 2 tablespoons, unsalted chopped

Peanut butter, 2 tablespoons

Soy sauce, 1 tablespoon

Cornstarch, 4 tablespoons

Angel hair pasta, 10 oz

Cooking Instructions:

1.Combine chicken, garlic and chicken stock in the pressure cooker. Close the lid and bring cooker to high temperature. When the maximum pressure is attained, lower heat and cook for 6 minutes. Remove from heat.

2.Release pressure either by quick or automatic method. Remove the lid and add red pepper, ginger, scallions and red pepper flakes. Cover loosely and cook for another five minutes.

3.In a separate bowl, mix peanut butter and soy sauce together. Add into the chicken mixture and cook for 3 minutes more.

4. Arrange cooked pasta in a platter, top with chicken and garnished with parsley and peanuts.

Chicken Porridge-Pressure Cooker Style

I really love this dish, because it combines chicken, rice and spices. I bet you would really want a second helping of this home-cooked goodness.

Preparation Time: 30 minutes

Cooking Time: 25 minutes

Number of Servings: 6

Ingredients:

Chicken breast, 3.5 lbs, skinless

White potatoes, 4 small size

Onions, 2 medium sized, chopped

Celery stalks, 2 medium sized, diced

Dried basil, ¼ teaspoon

Dried parsley, ¼ teaspoon

Thyme, 1/8 teaspoon

Cream of chicken soup, 1 can

Water, 2 cups

Pepper and salt to taste

Brown rice, cooked

Cooking Instructions:

1.Place chicken breasts and all other ingredients (except brown rice) into the pressure cooker.

2.Close the lid and bring cooker to high temperature. When the maximum pressure is attained, lower heat and cook for 25 minutes. Remove from heat and let pressure be released the natural way.

3. Open the lid and remove chicken. Debone the chicken and shred. Place chicken back into the cooker, add cooked rice and stir.

4. Serve while still hot.

Chicken Rice With Onions

This simple and easy to prepare meal will definitely awaken your taste buds.

Preparation Time: 10 minutes

Cooking Time: 10 minutes

Number of Servings: 4

Ingredients:

Cream of mushroom soup, 2 ½ cups

Chicken breast, 7ounces, boneless and skinless

White rice, 2 cups

Olive oil, 4 tablespoon

Onions, 2 tablespoons, chopped

Cooking Instructions:

1. In an uncovered pressure cooker, sauté onions in olive oil. Add chicken and cook for at least five minutes, or until brown.

3. Add rice, water and soup.

4. Close lid and bring cooker to high temperature. Cook for 10 minutes more.

5.Serve in bowls.

Pressurized Chicken Soup

This is really delicious, yet super simple. Prepare, pressurize, serve — just like that. The creamy consistency makes this delightful dish a hit for young and old alike.

Preparation Time: 10 minutes

Cooking Time: 25 minutes

Number of Servings: 4

Ingredients:

Chicken, 4 lbs, cut-up in serving sizes

Chicken stock, 2 cups

Bay leaf, 1 piece

Noodles, 8 oz

Cream of mushroom soup, 2 cans

Salt and pepper to taste

Cooking Instructions:

1. Place chicken in pressure cooker with enough water to cover half of the chicken. Cover the lid and pressurize for about 20 minutes. When done, release pressure using the natural method.

2. Cook noodles as per package instructions. Drain and set aside.

3. Mix 2 cans soup with 2 cups chicken stock. Add noodles and chicken into the soup. Simmer for 2 minutes. Remove from heat and serve.

Chicken With Thyme In Pressure Cooker

Easy to prepare, this meal is a combination of chicken meat and vegetables to satisfy your nutritional needs.

Preparation Time: 20 minutes

Cooking Time: 20 minutes

Number of Servings: 4

Ingredients:

Flour, 1 cup

Salt and pepper

Chicken breast, 2 pieces, cut into large pieces

Olive oil, 3 tablespoons

Onion, 1 medium size, sliced

Garlic, 2 cloves, crushed

Carrots, 4 large size, peeled and cut into large pieces

Celery, 2 sticks, sliced

Potatoes, 4 pieces, peeled and cut into serving pieces

Dried thyme, 1 tablespoon

Chicken stock, 2 cups

Parsley, ¼ cup, chopped

Cooking Instructions:

1.Roll chicken pieces in flour mixed with salt and pepper. Coat well.

2.In an uncovered pressure cooker, heat oil and fry chicken until golden brown.

3.Add onion, garlic and thyme to the chicken and cook for three minutes more.

4. Continue cooking with carrots, celery and potatoes added to the cooker. Cook for 3 minutes again.

5. Pour chicken stock into the pressure cooker and bring to boil, Ensure that no ingredients stick to the bottom of the pan.

6. Cover the lid of the cooker and bring to high temperature. Cook for 20 minutes.

7. Remove from heat and release pressure immediately.

8. Add the parsley and serve immediately.

BEEF RECIPES

Pressurized Beef Tips

This juicy beef recipe is something to look forward to, soft and tender to the bite and full of that beefy flavor everyone loves.

Preparation Time: 20 minutes

Cooking Time: 25 minutes

Number of Servings: 4-6

Ingredients:

All purpose flour, 3 tablespoons

Salt, 2 teaspoons

Black pepper, ½ teaspoons

Paprika, ½ teaspoon

Mustard powder, ¼ teaspoon

Vegetable oil, 2 tablespoons

Sirloin Steaks, 2 lbs, cubed

Garlic, 2 cloves, minced

Onions, 2 medium sizes, chopped

Beef consommé, 1 can (10 ½ oz)

Cooked rice, 4 cups

Cooking Instructions:

1.In a resealable plastic bag, mix together flour, salt, black pepper, paprika and mustard powder. Shake well. Add the beef cubes and shake until the cubes are fully coated.

2.Cook the beef cubes in vegetable oil until brown on all sides.

3.Add onions and garlic, sauté for 2 minutes then pour in the beef consommé.

4. Cover the pressure cooker tightly. Bring to high pressure and cook over medium heat for 25 minutes.

5.Remove from heat and release the pressure quickly. Open the lid and simmer for at least 3 minutes.

6. Serve over rice and enjoy.

Sweet And Sour Beef Spareribs

The common sweet and sour essences are made a little distinct in this recipe. Originally of Chinese origin, the many variations of this recipe makes each dish something to treasure.

Preparation Time: 15 minutes

Cooking Time: 20 minutes

Number of Servings: 4

Ingredients:

Short spareribs, 3 lb, cut into serving pieces

Vegetable oil, 3 tablespoons

Soy sauce, 3 tablespoons

Onion, 2 tablespoons, minced

Brown sugar, 2 tablespoons

Apricot marmalade, 2 tablespoons

Honey, 3 tablespoons

Cider vinegar, 2 tablespoons

Garlic, 3 cloves, minced

Dry sherry, 2 tablespoons

Ketchup, ¼ cup

Hot pepper sauce, 1 teaspoon

Cooking Instructions:

1. Except for the spareribs and vegetable oil, combine all ingredients in a small bowl. Set aside.

2. Heat oil in the pressure cooker and fry the spareribs until brown. Remove excess fat and stir in the sauce.

3. Close the lid tightly and cook for 15 minutes under high temperature.

4. Remove from heat and allow pressure to be released using the natural method. Remove the lid.

5. Transfer beef into a platter. Serve and enjoy!

Pressurized Beef Stroganoff

I simply love this beef dish. So tender to the bite, and made really special by the tasty sauce enveloping it.

Preparation Time: 15 minutes

Cooking Time: 25 minutes

Number of Servings: 4

Ingredients:

Beef stew meat or round steak, cut into 1" cubes

Fresh mushrooms, 1.4 lb, sliced

Vegetable oil, 3 tablespoons

Tomato paste, 2 tablespoons

Worcestershire sauce, 1 tablespoon

Flour, 2 tablespoons

Sour cream, 1 cup

Onion, 1 large size, chopped

Salt and pepper to taste

Garlic, 1 teaspoon, crushed

Beef broth, 1 cup

Egg noodles, 1 package, cooked

Cooking Instructions:

1. Heat oil in pressure cooker and fry meat until brown. Add flour and combine until evenly coated. Add onion, garlic powder, tomato paste, mushrooms, beef broth, salt, pepper and Worcestershire sauce. Mix thoroughly.

2. Close the lid and bring the pressure cooker to high temperature. Cook for 25 minutes on high pressure.

3. Remove from heat and allow pressure to release using the natural release method. Remove cover.

4. Add sour cream and mix well.

5. Serve over hot cooked egg noodles.

Hungarian Beef With Noodles

I just love the taste of beef in my egg noodles. Soft to the bite, tasty and nutritious, too. I wouldn't mind going for the second serving.

Preparation Time: 15 minutes

Cooking Time: 20 minutes

Number of Servings: 4

Ingredients:

Lean beef, ½ lb, cut into small pieces

Paprika, ½ teaspoon

Marjoram, ¼ teaspoon

Bacon, ½ cup, finely diced

Onions, 1 ½ cups, chopped

Caraway seeds, ¼ teaspoon, crushed

Potatoes, 2 medium sizes, chopped

Water, 1 ¼ cup

Salt to taste

Egg noodles, 1 package, cooked

Cooking Instructions:

1. In the pressure cooker, sauté bacon. Add paprika and water. Stir.

2. Add beef, marjoram, potatoes, salt, onions and crushed caraway seeds.

3. Close the lid tightly and bring to high temperature. Cook for 15 minutes.

4. Remove from heat and release pressure. Serve immediately with hot egg noodles.

Beef Pot Roast The Easy Way

Over many other beef pot roast recipes, this is my favorite. It is super easy to prepare and cook. Give it a try.

Preparation Time: 15 minutes

Cooking Time: 40 minutes

Number of Servings: 3 to 4

Ingredients:

Pot roast, 1.5 lb

Canola oil, 3 tablespoons

Onion, 1 medium size, chopped

Bay leaf, 1 medium size

Beef stock, 1 ½ cups

Salt and pepper to taste

Cooking Instructions:

1.Brown roast in canola oil in the pressure cooker. Place in trivet in the cooker Add chopped onion, bay leaf and beef stock. Season with salt and pepper.

2. Close the lid tightly and bring to high temperature. Cook for 35 minutes.

3. Remove from heat and release pressure. Serve.

Pressurized Classic Stew O' Beef

This quick and easy recipe is a delicious combination of beef, veggies and seasonings. Perfect for those cold and sleepy mornings.

Preparation Time: 10 minutes

Cooking Time: 30 minutes

Number of Servings: 6

Ingredients:

Beef chuck, 3 lbs, cut into 1" chunks

Olive oil, 1 tablespoon

Tomato paste, 3 tablespoons

Celery, ¾ cup, finely diced

Carrot, ¾ cup, finely diced

Onions, 1 ½ cups, coarsely chopped

Red wine, ½ cup

Frozen peas, 1 cup

Beef broth, 3/4 cup

Bay leaves, 2 large sizes

Black pepper, fresh ground

Fresh thyme, 2 teaspoons

Cornstarch, 2 teaspoons

Balsamic vinegar, 2 teaspoons

Cooking Instructions:

1. In an uncovered pressure cooker, Sauté in oil the onions, celery and carrots. Add wine and tomato paste. Simmer until only about half of the liquid is left, approximately five minutes.

2. Add beef, broth and bay leaf.

3. Close the lid tightly and bring to high temperature. Cook for 16 minutes.

3. Remove from heat and release pressure naturally for about 10 minutes.

4. Open the cover of the cooker and discard any fat. Mix in thyme, salt and pepper. For a more flavorful broth, add a little vinegar.

5. For a thicker stew, blend cornstarch with 2 tablespoons water. Add to hot stew and simmer up to the desired consistency. Add peas and simmer for another minute.

6. Remove from heat and serve.

Beef Brisket Chinese Style

This dish oozes with flavors of onions, ginger, and Chinese marinade. Delightfully tasty!

Preparation Time: 25 minutes plus 8 hours chilling time

Cooking Time: 20 minutes

Number of Servings: 6

Ingredients:

Beef brisket joint, 1.7 lbs

Ginger, 4 slices

Spring onions, 2 medium sizes, quartered

Cooking oil, 1 tablespoon

Lee Kum Kee Chinese marinade, 1 cup

Water, 7 cups

Rock sugar to taste

Cooking Instructions:

1.Prepare the brisket by boiling it for ten minutes. Rinse with cold water and drain. Set aside.

2.In a frying pan, stir fry in oil the ginger and spring onions for 2 minutes. Transfer into the pressure cooker and add the brisket, Chinese marinade, sugar and water. Cook in high pressure for seven minutes.

3. Remove from heat and release pressure using the quick release method. Transfer the brisket to a serving platter and cool. Put in the fridge and chill overnight.

4. Slice and serve.

Pressurized Chili Con Carne

This is a well-loved dish all over the world. Although many variations have been made to suit everyone's tastes, one thing remains, it is an all-time favorite.

Preparation Time: 30 minutes

Cooking Time: 30 minutes

Number of Servings: 4

Ingredients:

Ground beef, 0.88 lb.

Canned tomatoes, 10.75 oz, drained and chopped

Tomato paste, 1 teaspoon

Olive oil, 4 tablespoons

Kidney beans, 5.3 oz, soaked

Onion, 1 medium size, chopped

Garlic, 2 cloves, finely chopped

Bay leaf, 1 medium size

Chili powder, 1 tablespoon

Salt, 1 teaspoon

Ground cumin, ½ teaspoon

Basil leaves, dried

Water, 3/4

Cooking Instructions:

1.In the pressure cooker, cook ground beef in a tablespoon of oil until brown. Transfer into a platter.

2.Add in the remaining oil and stir fry garlic and onions. Add beef and the other ingredients. Mix well.

3.Close the lid of the pressure cooker and bring to high temperature. Cook for 18 minutes.

4.Remove from heat and let cool. Allow pressure to be released naturally.

5.Open the lid and remove the bay leaves.

6. Serve while hot.

Juicy Yummy Corned Beef
Who doesn't love corned beef? It can be enjoyed as a dish or as sandwich filler. Nutritionally satisfying without so much preparation fuss.

Preparation Time: 60 minutes

Cooking Time: 60 minutes

Number of Servings: 6

Ingredients:

Beef brisket, 4.4 lb

Celery, 0.75 lb, sliced

Oranges, 2 small sizes, sliced unpeeled

Onions, 2 small sizes, sliced thinly

Garlic, 2 cloves, chopped

Bay leaves, 3 small sizes, halved

Dill, 1 tablespoon

Cinnamon, 4 sticks, halved

Water, 2 1/4 cups

Cooking Instructions:

1.Soak beef brisket in water for one hour. Drain before cooking.

2.In the pressure cooker, place the beef brisket. Add the remaining ingredients. Add water until it just covers the top of the beef.

3.Close the lid tightly and bring to high temperature. Cook meat for 50 minutes.

4.Remove from heat and allow the pressure to be released naturally. After the pressure has been totally released, open the cover and transfer beef to a serving dish, cool for 5 minutes.

5.Cut thinly, and serve.

Tasty Beef Curry

This tasty recipe is finger-licking delicious. Serve with steamed rice for that completely enticing meal.

Preparation Time: 15 minutes

Cooking Time: 20 minutes

Number of Servings: 4

Ingredients:

Chuck steak beef, 1.1 lb, diced

Olive oil, 3 tablespoons

Potatoes, 2 to 3 large pieces, diced

Mild curry powder, 2 ½ tablespoons

Grainy wine mustard, 1 tablespoon

Onions, 2 large sizes, chopped

Garlic, 2 cloves, chopped

Coconut milk, 1 can

Tomato sauce, 1 jar

Cooking Instructions:

1. In the pressure cooker, sauté onions and garlic in olive oil. Add potatoes and mustard and cook for another minute.

2. Add beef and fry until brown.

3. Stir in curry powder, tomato sauce and coconut milk.

4. Close lid of the pressure cooker, and set to high temperature. Cook for 10 minutes.

5. Remove from heat and allow pressure to be released naturally.

6. Transfer contents into a bowl and serve with steamed rice.

Zesty Spanish Beef With Pureed Vegetables

Use the pressure cooker for this quick meal that is distinctly Spanish. Easy to prepare and tasty to the palate.

Preparation Time: 15 minutes

Cooking Time: 45 minutes

Number of Servings: 8-10

Ingredients:

Beef rolled joint, 3.3 lb

Olive oil, 3½ tablespoons

Bay leaves, 2 medium sizes

Garlic, 4 cloves, chopped

Salt to taste

Carrots, 4 medium sizes, chopped

Onions, 2 medium sizes, chopped

Tomatoes, 3 medium sizes, chopped

Brandy, 1 small glass

Cooking Instructions:

1.Season beef with salt. Set aside.

2.In the pressure cooker, cook bay leaves in oil, add garlic and sauté for one or two minutes. Remove and discard bay leaves.

3.Fry beef in the same oil in the cooker until brown. Remove and set aside.

4.Sauté onions in the same oil in the cooker until soft. Add carrots and cook for five minutes. Add tomatoes and cook for another five minutes. Stir constantly to avoid sticking at the bottom of the pan.

5. Add the beef back to the cooker. Put in brandy and a glass of water. Cover the lid, bring to pressure and cook for 30 minutes.

6. Remove from heat and let pressure come out naturally from the cooker for about 10 to 15 minutes. Remove the beef and set aside.

7. Use a hand-held blender to puree the vegetable mixture in the pressure cooker. Simmer again for a thicker consistency.

8. Slice the beef into thin pieces and arrange in a platter. Serve with vegetable puree on top.

SEAFOOD

One Pot Fish Chowder

Try this easy, tasty, deliciously creamy and filling fish chowder.

Preparation Time: 15 minutes

Cooking Time: 25 minutes

Number of Servings: 4-6

Ingredients:

Haddock or any other white fish, 1.1 lb, skinless and boneless, cut into medium chunks

Potatoes, 0.75 lb, cut into medium chunks

Onion, 1 small piece, chopped

Milk, 1½ cups

Chicken stock or broth, 2 cups

Water, 2 cups

Half and half, 2 cups

Salt and pepper to taste

Cooking Instructions:

1.In the pressure cooker, combine fish, onion, chicken stock, water and milk. Cover lid and bring to medium-high heat pressure. Cook for eight minutes.

2.Remove from heat and release pressure naturally.

3. Return the cooker to continue cooking, with lid uncovered. Add half and half and stir continuously until soup has slightly thickened. Season with salt and pepper.

4.Remove from heat and garnish as needed. Serve and enjoy!

Fish And Orange-Ginger Sauce

The natural flavor of fish comes out specially with ginger and citrus! Definitely, you'll want to taste this delectable fish recipe that I personally like, too. So healthy and delicious.

Preparation Time: 10 minutes

Cooking Time: 7 minutes

Number of Servings: 4

Ingredients:

White fish fillets, 4 pieces

Orange, 1 medium size, juiced

Ginger, 1 thumb-sized piece

Spring onions, 4 pieces

White wine, 1 cup

Olive oil

Salt and pepper

Cooking Instructions:

1.Dry fish fillets using paper towels.

2.Rub olive oil in fillets, and season with salt and pepper.

3.In the pressure cooker, add white wine, ginger, spring onions, and orange juice. Place fish in the steamer basket, and cover the lid. Bring the cooker to high temperature and cook for 7 minutes.

4.Remove from heat and release steam naturally. Arrange fish in a platter, or you garnish with green vegetables. Pour sauce over the fish and serve immediately.

Steamed Fillet-O-Fish

This healthy and flavorful dish is so simple to make, in less than 15 minutes.

Preparation Time: 10 minutes

Cooking Time: 5 minutes

Number of Servings: 4

Ingredients:

Fish fillets, 4 pieces

Olives, 1 cup

Garlic, 1 clove, crushed

Cherry tomatoes, 1.1 lb, sliced

Fresh thyme, 1 large pinch

Olive oil

Water, 1 cup

Salt and pepper to taste

Cooking Instructions:

1. Heat the pressure cooker. Add a cup of water.

2. Arrange fish fillets in the steaming basket, all in one layer. Add sliced cherry tomatoes and olives on top of the fillets. On another layer, add some fresh thyme, crushed garlic, olive oil, and salt.

3. Place the steaming basket inside the pressure cooker. Close the lid and bring the cooker to high temperature. Cook fillets for 3 to 5 minutes on high pressure.

4. Remove from heat and release pressure naturally.

5. Arrange fillets in a platter, sprinkle with the remaining thyme, olive oil, salt and pepper. Serve.

Spicy Fish Curry In Coconut Sauce

Originally from India, curry dishes have evolved and have been enhanced by different cooking styles. This dish combines curry's two most common ingredients, fish and coconut. Perfect for lunch or dinner, its rich and classic flavor will surely make your mealtime enjoyable and memorable.

Preparation Time: 10 minutes

Cooking Time: 5 minutes

Number of Servings: 4-6

Ingredients:

Fish fillets, 1.65 lb, cut in bite size pieces

Tomato, 1 medium size, chopped

Coconut milk, 2 cups, unsweetened

Onions, 2 medium sizes, chopped into strips

Hot chili, 2 medium sizes, cut into strips

Garlic, 2 cloves, minced

Curry leaves, 6 pieces

Ginger, 1 tablespoon, freshly grated

Ground coriander, 1 tablespoon

Ground cumin, 2 teaspoons

Ground turmeric, ½ teaspoon

Hot pepper flakes, 1 teaspoon

Ground fenugreek, ½ teaspoon

Lemon juice

Salt

Cooking Instructions:

1. In an uncovered pressure cooker, heat oil on medium-low heat. leaves and fry for 1 minute. Add onion, ginger and garlic. Sauté unt

2. Add the spices – coriander, turmeric, cumin, fenugreek and hot pe Continue to sauté for 2 more minutes.

3. Pour in the coconut milk, stirring continuously to prevent sticking at bottom of the cooker.

4. Add hot chili, tomatoes and fish. Stir until the mixture covers the fish fi thoroughly.

5. Close the lid of the cooker and bring to high pressure. Cook for 5 minutes.

6. Remove from heat and release pressure using the quick release method.

7. Transfer dish into a platter, season with salt and lemon juice on top. Serve immediately.

Steamy Steamed Salmon

Try a bite of this steamed salmon done the Italian way. The fish is steamed using its own juices, with vegetables and spices added.

Preparation Time: 10 minutes

Cooking Time: 5 minutes

Number of Servings: 4

Ingredients:

Salmon fillets, 4 pieces

Tomatoes, 3 medium sizes, sliced

White onion, 1 medium size, sliced thinly

Parsley, 4 sprigs

Add curry
soft.

pper.

the

oil, arrange the following in order: a teaspoon of oil,
per, oil, fish fillets, salt, pepper, oil, parsley, thyme, onion,
and oil.

lets

oil and wrap thoroughly. Set aside.

pressure cooker, pour two cups of water. Position the steamer in the
, and place two foil-wrapped fish. Cook two fish at a time.

Close the lid of the cooker, bring to high temperature. Cook in low heat for
2 minutes.

5.Release the pressure using quick release method. However, take the foil-wrapped fish only after about five minutes.

6. Remove from foil and transfer into a platter. Serve.

Steamed Fish-Mediterranean Style

Here's something different for steamed fish — tomatoes and capers. The result will surprise you, Its sweet and sour taste is a welcome change from the usual citrus flavor.

Preparation Time: 5 minutes

Cooking Time: 5 minutes

Number of Servings: 4

Ingredients:

White fish fillet, 4 pieces

Cherry tomatoes, 1.1 lb, halved

Olives, 1 cup

Thyme

Olive oil

Garlic, 1 clove, crushed

Capers, 2 tablespoons, pickled

Salt and pepper

Cooking Instructions:

1.In a heatproof bowl (Pyrex), place in layer the following: cherry tomatoes, fresh thyme, fish, crushed garlic, salt and olive oil.

2. Put the bowl in the pressure cooker.

3. Close the lid of the cooker, bring to high temperature. Cook in low heat for 5 minutes.

4. Remove from heat and release pressure using the natural method.

5. Serve in a platter by garnishing with more cherry tomatoes and olives.

Potatoes And Octopus Medley

Who says that octopus is tough? Not with the pressure cooker to the rescue. There is, however, a secret to making it so tender to the bite. With this recipe, you'll never be sorry you tried it.

Preparation Time: 20 minutes

Cooking Time: 35 minutes

Number of Servings: 6

Ingredients:

Octopus, 2.2 lbs

Potatoes, 2.2 lbs

Garlic, 3 cloves, crushed

Bay leaf, 1 piece

Peppercorns, ½ teaspoon

Vinegar, 5 tablespoons

Parsley, chopped

Olive oil, 1/2 cup

Salt and pepper

Cooking Instructions:

1. Clean the octopus well; remove the head, all of its contents, including eyes and beak. Cut in half and clean the insides. Rinse under running water and set aside.

2. Wash potatoes thoroughly without removing the skin. Put them unpeeled in the pressure cooker. Add enough water to cover half of the potatoes. Add salt for a bit of flavor. Close the lid and bring the cooker to high pressure. Cook for 15 minutes.

3. Remove from heat and release pressure using quick release method. Transfer the potatoes in another container using tongs. Do not discard the liquid from the pressure cooker.

4. Peel the potatoes while they are still hot. Set aside.

5. Add more water to the pressure cooker up to the amount you think is needed to submerge the octopus. Add bay leaf, garlic, pepper and salt. Bring to a boil.

6. When it reaches boiling point, add the octopus, with the tentacles at the bottom of the cooker. Close the lid and let the cooker reach high temperature. Cook for 20 minutes or more until tender.

7. Remove from heat, drain liquid and chop octopus into bite-sized pieces. Set aside.

8. Chop the potatoes in bite size pieces.

9. To prepare vinaigrette, mix olive oil, 2 garlic clove, vinegar, salt and pepper in a small jar. Close the jar and shake to thoroughly blend the ingredients.

10. Mix all ingredients together in a bowl. Garnish with parsley. Cover tightly and chill in the fridge before serving.

Pressure Cooker Seafood Chowder

How would you like this tasty treat? This is something you will really love, definitely!

Preparation Time: 10 minutes

Cooking Time: 10 minutes

Number of Servings: 4-6

Ingredients:

White fish, 1 lb, cut into bite-size pieces

Butter, 2 tablespoons

Fish broth or clam juice, 4 cups

Leeks, 2 large pieces, sliced

Water, 2 cups

Potatoes, 6 medium sized, peeled and diced

Dried thyme, ½ teaspoon

Heavy cream, ½ cup

Bay leaf, 1 piece

Salt and pepper to taste

Cooking Instructions:

1. Heat and melt butter in an uncovered pressure cooker. Sauté leeks, and stir in water, broth, and potatoes. Add bay leaf, salt and pepper.

2. Close lid and bring to high pressure. Cook for 4 minutes. Remove from heat and release pressure quickly.

3. Open the lid and remove the bay leaf. Return cooker to medium heat. Add fish and simmer for 3 minutes. Add thyme and cream. Stir occasionally for another 3 minutes.

4. Remove from heat and serve in bowls.

Seafood And Crouton Delight

Something about this dish will remind you that food need not be too exquisitely prepared to be enjoyed. Simple pleasures of life come in the form of good food like this.

Preparation Time: 5 minutes

Cooking Time: 26 minutes

Number of Servings: 4

Ingredients:

Tomatoes, 3 medium sizes, scalded, peeled and sliced

Squid, 1.7 lb, sliced

Garlic, 1 clove, crushed

Onion, 1 medium size

Thyme, 2 sticks

Fennel, 2 sticks

Parsley, ½ teaspoon, minced

Stale bread, 4 slices

Dry white wine, 6 tablespoons

Extra virgin olive oil, 4 tablespoon

Salt and pepper to taste

Cooking Instructions:

1. Pour 3 tablespoons of oil in the pressure cooker. Sauté onions and add the squids. Sauté for another 3 minutes.

2. Add tomatoes, wine and herbs. Stir and close the lid. Cook under high pressure for 20 minutes.

3. Remove from heat and allow pressure to escape using the quick release method. Remove and discard fennel and thyme sticks. Season with salt and pepper.

4. To make garlic croutons, rub bread slices with garlic cloves, and dice them. Toast in oil until brown.

5. Spoon squid into bowls and top with croutons. Serve hot.

Fish Fillets In Pickle Sauce

Fish fillets usually have similar taste, but the difference lies in the sauce used for dipping. This dish would make you want to try another batch of fish fillets, with the same sauce of course!

Preparation Time: 10 minutes

Cooking Time: 8 minutes

Number of Servings: 4

Ingredients:

Bay leaves, 2 pieces

Anchovy paste, ½ tablespoon

Trout, 4 pieces

Dry tarragon, ½ tablespoon

Dry parsley, ½ tablespoon

Mustard, 1 tablespoon

Pickles, 2 pieces

Fish broth, 2 tablespoons

Mustard, 3/4 cup

Water, 4 1/4 cup

Salt and pepper to taste

Cooking Instructions:

1.Place the trout in the pressure cooker. Add 4 1/4 cups of water, broth and bay leaf. Season with salt and pepper.

2.Close the lid and pressurize the fish. Cook for 5 minutes after the cooker made a hissing sound. Remove from heat and allow steam to escape naturally. Open the lid and let cool.

3. Carefully take out the fish from the cooker. Place in a platter.

4. To prepare the sauce, drain pickles, mince and place in a bowl. Add mayonnaise, herbs and anchovy paste and mustard . Mix well until a smooth consistency is obtained. Transfer the sauce in a small bowl.

5. Serve the trout with the sauce on the side.

Creamy Salmon In Mushrooms

The dish speaks for itself, yummy salmon with the best combination of mushroom. So temptingly enticing and truly something worth trying.

Preparation Time: 50 minutes

Cooking Time: 25 minutes

Number of Servings: 4

Ingredients:

Salmon, 1.8 lbs, sliced

Dry mushrooms, 1.7 oz

Flour, 2 tablespoons

Dry dill, 1 tablespoon

Milk, 1/2 cup

Shallots, 2 pieces, minced

Dry white wine, 6 tablespoons

Extra virgin olive oil, 3 tablespoons

Cooking Instructions:

1.Soak mushrooms in hot water for 30 minutes. Squeeze excess water.

2.Heat oil in the cooker, add shallots and sauté for 20 minutes. Add mushrooms, and lightly fry. Add the white wine, and cook until liquid evaporates almost completely.

3. Add salmon slices and brown on both sides. Add milk, water and flour. Season with salt and pepper.

4.Close the lid and let pressure build up to high heat. Cook for 5 minutes. Remove from heat and allow steam to release. Open the lid and transfer the salmon and mushrooms to a platter. Pour over the sauce, garnish with dill. Yummy!

VEGETABLES

Saucy Asparagus Delight

This vegetable recipe is a delightful side dish to savory meat dishes. The sauce makes it all the more special.

Preparation Time: 10 minutes

Cooking Time: 10 minutes

Number of Servings: 4

Ingredients:

Eggs, 6 medium sizes, hard boiled

Parsley, 1 bunch

Red wine, 4 tablespoons

Mustard, 2 tablespoons

Asparagus, 2.2 lbs

Red wine vinegar, 1/2 cup

Extra virgin olive oil, 1 cup

Cooking Instructions:

1.Peel asparagus and remove the hard parts. Steam cook them in the pressure cooker with 1 ½ cup of water. Cook for 6 minutes once it reaches the maximum heat.

2. Remove from heat and release pressure. Open the lid and transfer asparagus to a platter. Let cool.

3. To prepare the sauce, remove the shell of the hardboiled eggs, separate the whites from the yolks. Crush yolks with a fork, and while stirring constantly, gradually add oil and the vinegar. Dilute mustard in the red wine vinegar and mix with the sauce.

4. Arrange asparagus in a round dish, season with salt, and cover with the sauce. Serve immediately.

Potatoes In Herbs

Perfect as garnishing for fish and roasts, most especially in mixed veggies. Try and see for yourself!

Preparation Time: 5 minutes

Cooking Time: 10 minutes

Number of Servings: 4

Ingredients:

Potatoes, 2.2 lbs

Butter, 4 tablespoons

Salt and pepper to taste

Flour, ½ tablespoon

Garlic, 1 clove

Nutmeg, 1 pinch

Parsley, 1 tablespoon, minced

Milk, 2 cups

Cooking Instructions:

1.Combine garlic and parsley. Mix and set aside.

2.Peel the potatoes, wash and dry them. Cut into serving sizes and place in the pressure cooker.

3. Season with pepper and salt. Add milk.

4. Cover the pressure cooker. Bring to maximum temperature and cook for 5 minutes.

5. Remove from heat and allow the pressure to be released using the quick release method.

6. In a saucepan, melt butter and while constantly stirring, add the sifted flour.

7.Transfer this mix to the potatoes, Add garlic, nutmeg, and parsley. Stir well.

8. Transfer potato in a serving dish and serve immediately.

Zucchini And Green Beans Galore

Greenish and healthy, this is a welcome dish to those who want a nutritious meal anytime of the day.

Preparation Time: 15 minutes

Cooking Time: 10 minutes

Number of Servings: 4

Ingredients:

Scallion, 4 stalks

Fresh tarragon, 1 tablespoon

Arugula, 3 leaves

Green beans, 10.6 oz

Zucchini, 3 pieces

Tender spinach, 3 leaves

Garlic, 1 clove

Salt and pepper

Mustard, 1 tablespoon

Red wine vinegar, 2 tablespoon

Extra virgin olive oil, 4 tablespoons

Cooking Instructions:

1.Prepare the vegetables by removing the threads and ends of green beans and by washing the zucchini.

2.Place the vegetables in the steam cooking basket in the pressure cooker. Add 1 cup of water. Close the lid, and pressurize the vegetables for 4 minutes. Drain and reserve.

3.In a jar, mix together oil, vinegar, mustard, salt and pepper. Close jar cap and shake well to mix.

4. Wash and dry arugula, spinach, scallions and tarragons. Place inside a food processor and blend until a very fine consistency results. Mix well with the prepared vinaigrette.

5. Cut green beans in small pieces and arrange them in a serving dish. Add in the sliced zucchini. Pour some of the sauce and serve immediately.

All-Star German Potato Salad

Combined with bacon, this potato salad is an all-time favorite of health aficionados. Why not make it your favorite, too?

Preparation Time: 10 minutes

Cooking Time: 2 minutes

Number of Servings: 4

Ingredients:

Bacon, 4 slices

Sugar, 4 teaspoons

Vinegar, 3 tablespoons

Mustard, 1 teaspoons

Potatoes, 4 medium large in ¼" slices

Onion, 1 medium size, sliced thinly

Salt and pepper

Celery seed, ½ teaspoon

Cooking Instructions:

1.Fry bacon in the pressure cooker until crisp. Drain on paper towels and crumble. Reserve the bacon drippings.

2.Rinse the pressure cooker to remove bacon drippings. Add 1 ¾ cups water into the pressure cooker.

3. In a small bowl, mix together the sugar, mustard, vinegar and bacon drippings.

4.In the pressure cooker basket, arrange the potatoes and onions in layers. Season with salt, pepper, celery seed, vinegar-mustard mixture and crumbled bacon.

5.Lock the lid of the cooker and bring to maximum pressure. Cook for 2 minutes on high pressure.

6. Remove from heat and allow pressure to come out using either the quick release method or the automatic release method.

7. Lift out the cooker basket, transfer contents to a platter, and serve.

Bloody Cabbage Salad

This German salad is a good source of Vitamin C, fiber and antioxidants. And it is so easy to make with the help of the pressure cooker.

Preparation Time: 5 minutes

Cooking Time: 2 minutes

Number of Servings: 4

Ingredients:

Red cabbage, 2 cups, shredded

Onion, ¼ cup, chopped

Canola oil, 1 tablespoon

Red wine vinegar, 1 to 2 teaspoons

Brown sugar, ½ teaspoon

Salt and pepper

Cooking Instructions:

1.Put red cabbage in a steamer basket. Lock the lid of the cooker and bring to pressure. Cook for 1 to 2 minutes under high pressure.

2. Remove from heat and release pressure immediately.

3. Lift the steamer basket and run cold water over the cabbage.

4. Arrange cabbage in a platter, and add the remaining ingredients. Mix and serve. If desired, you may add more oil and vinegar.

Fiesta Pasta Sauce

With this recipe, you need not worry about the long hour spent on simmering your pasta sauce.

Preparation Time: 5 minutes

Cooking Time: 12 minutes

Number of Servings: 4

Ingredients:

Canola oil, 3 tablespoons

Onion. ½ cup finely chopped

Carrot, ¾ cup, finely chopped

Celery, ¾ cup, finely chopped

Garlic, 2 cloves, minced

Canned tomatoes, 1 large can, crushed

Dried basil, 3 teaspoons

Dried oregano, 2 teaspoons

Dried parsley, 1 teaspoon

Bay leaves, 1 or 2 pieces

Dry red or white wine, ¼ cup

Water, ½ cup

Salt and pepper to taste

Cooking Instructions:

1.Heat oil in the pressure cooker. Sauté onions, carrot, celery, and garlic. Put all the remaining ingredients together in the cooker. Lock the lid and bring to high pressure. Cook for 10 minutes on high pressure.

2. Remove from heat and allow pressure to be released using the quick release method. Serve with pasta.

Potato With Bean Casserole

Very easy and flavorful, this will surely make your meal more enjoyable.

Preparation Time: 5 minutes

Cooking Time: 5 minutes

Number of Servings: 4

Ingredients:

Potatoes, 3 medium sizes, peeled and cut in 1" cubes

Green beans, ¾ lb

Olive oil, 1 tablespoon

Onion, 1 medium size, minced

Green pepper, 1 medium size, diced

Parsley, 1 tablespoon, minced

Salt and pepper to taste

Cooking Instructions:

1.Mix all ingredients together in the pressure cooker.

2.Lock the lid and bring to high pressure. Cook for 3 minutes. Remove from heat and release pressure using quick release method.

3. Serve and enjoy!

Pressurized Potato Soup

A deliciously heartwarming soup made in your own home.

Preparation Time: 10 minutes

Cooking Time: 8 minutes

Number of Servings: 4

Ingredients:

Celery, ¾ cup, chopped

Carrots, ¾ cup, chopped

Potatoes, ¾ cup, chopped

Chicken broth 4 cups

Milk, 1 cup

Chicken bouillon

Parsley, 1 sprig

Salt and pepper

Cooking Instructions:

1.Place celery, carrots, potatoes and chicken broth in the cooker. Close the lid and bring to high pressure. Cook for 4 minutes.

2. Open the pressure cooker after releasing the pressure using the quick release method.

3.Cool slightly.

4. Using food processor, make a puree of about half of the vegetables. Return the vegetables and add bouillon, parsley, milk, salt and pepper.

6. Serve and enjoy.

Steamed Cauliflower In Coconut Sauce

The exotic taste of coconut sauce is temptingly delicious and nutritious.

Preparation Time: 15 minutes

Cooking Time: 5 minutes

Number of Servings: 4-6

Ingredients:

Fresh green beans, 1 cup, sliced into bite size pieces

Cauliflower, 1 small head, cut into florets

Fresh dill, 2 tablespoons, chopped

Coconut milk, ½ cup

Turmeric, 1 pinch

Lemon juice, 1 tablespoon

Salt and pepper to taste

Cooking Instructions:

1. In a mixing bowl, combine dill, coconut milk, turmeric, lemon juice and season with salt and pepper. Mix and refrigerate for at least one hour.

2. Put the vegetables in the steamer basket. Place inside the pressure cooker. Close the lid and bring to high temperature. Cook for 5 minutes.

3. Remove from heat and release pressure using the quick method. Arrange vegetables in a platter. Pour sauce over them and serve immediately.

Pressure Cooker Vegetarian Beans

This recipe is prepared with vegetarians in mind. No meat whatsoever, but with flavor so full, you will definitely get hooked to this.

Preparation Time: 15 minutes plus 8 hours soaking time

Cooking Time: 50 minutes

Number of Servings: 10

Ingredients:

Dry pinto beans, 2 cups

Garlic, 2 cloves, crushed

Dry cilantro, 1 tablespoon

Yellow onion, 1 medium size

Cumin, ¼ teaspoon

Pepper, ¼ teaspoon

Chili pepper powder, 1 teaspoon

Salt to taste

Water, 6 quarts

Cooking Instructions:

1. Soak beans overnight in 4 cups of water.

2. Drain beans and transfer into the pressure cooker.

3. Add remaining ingredients.

4. Close lid and bring to high pressure. Cook for 50 minutes.

5. Remove from heat and release pressure using the quick release method.

6. Transfer beans to serving bowls.

Crunchy Lemony Broccoli

As a side dish or a meal in itself, broccoli is simply delicious.

Preparation Time: 10 minutes

Cooking Time: 3 minutes

Number of Servings: 6

Ingredients:

Broccoli, 2 lbs, cut into florets

Lemon, 4 slices

Water, 1/2 cup

Salt and pepper to taste

Cooking Instructions:

1.Prepare the pressure cooker by adding 1/2 cup of water. Add broccoli and lemon juice. Season with salt and pepper.

2. Close the lid of the cooker and bring to high temperature. Cook for a minute.

3. Remove from heat and release pressure using the quick release method.

4. Serve.

END OF BOOK 1

BOOK 2

Electric Pressure Cooker Cookbook

Vol. 2 54 Electric Pressure Cooker Recipes
(Breakfast, Brunch, Appetizers And Desserts)

ROSA BARNES

INTRODUCTION

Have A Great Day With Pressure Cooked Meals

The fantastic advantages of the pressure cooker are known by a lot of people but many of them still restrict its usage to cooking dinner when pressed for time. Dinner is considered to be the most important meal of the day but breakfast is equally as vital to healthy living. When you eat a full breakfast, you will not have to eat a heavy lunch and this helps you to avoid junk food and snacks when you are at work or on the road. You also have adequate energy to do a lot of work during the day when you eat a light brunch at midday.

Why not start using your electric pressure cooker for cooking breakfast before leaving home in the mornings? The Electric Pressure Cooker Cookbook Vol. 2 is a compilation of quick and easy recipes for Breakfast, Brunch, Appetizers And Desserts. Even if you don't wake up too early, the quick cooking time of the recipes using your pressure cooker will get a hot meal ready on your table in just a few minutes. You could also prepare something to take to work within the same time span.

The recipes in this book are not only for fast cooking, they are also easy to make even for inexperienced cooks. Electric cookers are really great for making pancakes, omelets and other breakfast dishes you are used to. The appetizers and desserts you will make will also be delightful. Whether you want to braise, fry or sear food, your pressure cooker is up to the task. Indulge your family in a meal of eggs, sausage, bacon, sweet chocolate or any other favorites. Throw in vegetables and the seasonings you love to create a delicious dish.

Cooking With Your Electric Pressure Cooker

In the earlier days, the pressure cooker has been known to soften tough cuts of meats and other foods which need to be softened for food, all for a shorter period of time to cook. The resulting dishes are soft, tender and really tasty – cooked to perfection, as they say.

Many stories have also been told about accidents when using pressure cookers, leading to the thinking that while this kitchen gadget is helpful to us, there are certain disadvantages that cannot be overlooked.

As time progressed, we have noticed improvements and various enhancements to the kitchen gadget. Added safety features have been designed to minimize kitchen mishaps, while the resulting dish is, as expected, tender and tasty.

It is every homemaker's dream to go through the day doing chores without much of a hitch, especially in food preparation. It is not a joke to work in the kitchen for at least three times a day wishing that there could be another way to prepare meals the easy and convenient way.

That is why most homemakers like me really rely on useful kitchen gadgets such as the electric pressure cooker. With its advance features and enhancements, we can cook virtually almost anything. You can make pressure-cooker staples such as roasts, stews and casseroles. What's more, it can cook to perfection vegetables, rice, beans, and even delightful desserts such as custards and puddings.

Having an electric pressure cooker is really a wise investment for a smart homemaker. If you don't own one yet, or if you are contemplating of buying one, follow your instinct and grab one now.

BREAKFAST

Very Early Hash Browns

Enjoy these hash browns just as the sun rises.

Preparation Time: 5 minutes

Cooking Time: 15 minutes

Number of Servings: 4

Ingredients:

8 ounces ground sausages

½ cup water

1 lb country style hash browns

4 eggs, large sizes, lightly beaten

1 cup grated cheddar cheese

Directions:

1. Brown sausages in the pressure cooker until cooked through, and then break them apart.

2. Remove the excess oil from the cooker. Add water and stir with the sausages, gently scraping off meat from the bottom of the cooker.

3. Add the hash browns and egg over the sausage mixture.

4. Close the lid of the cooker and bring to low pressure. Cook for 4 minutes.

5. Remove from heat and remove pressure using the quick release method.

6. Open the lid, sprinkle cheese evenly over the hash, and cover the cooker once again. Let stand for 5 minutes for the cheese to melt.

7. Serve immediately in individual dishes.

Nutritious Irish Oatmeal

Also called steel-cut oats, these are high in Vitamin B, protein, calcium, and fiber. Nutritious and delicious!

Preparation Time: 5 minutes

Cooking Time: 8 minutes

Number of Servings: 4

Ingredients:

4 cups water

1 cup steel-cut oats, toasted

A pinch of salt

1 tablespoon butter

Directions:

1.Place the rack inside the cooker and pour ½ cup of water.

2.Combine together in a metal bowl the following: oats, salt, butter and the remaining water. Place bowl on top of the rack.

3.Close the lid of the cooker and bring to medium temperature. Cook for five minutes. For creamy oatmeal, cook for eight minutes.

4.Remove from heat and release pressure using the slow release method. Open the lid and remove the metal bowl using tongs.

5.Serve in individual bowls, adjusting the flavor according to your taste.

Yummy Breakfast Vegetable

This medley of vegetables provide you the needed nutrients for your busy day.

Preparation Time: 5 minutes

Cooking Time: 12 minutes

Number of Servings: 4

Ingredients:

1 onion, diced

2 carrots, diced

2 potatoes, diced

1 stalk celery, diced

1 red bell pepper, diced

1 cup squash, diced

2 tomatoes, diced

1 tablespoon oil

1 tablespoon soy sauce

¼ cup water

Black pepper to taste

Directions:

1.In the pressure cooker, sauté onion in oil for two minutes. Add potatoes, carrots, celery and bell pepper. Sauté for another 2 minutes then add water and soy sauce.

2. Close the lid of the pressure cooker and bring to high temperature. Cook for 2 minutes.

3.Remove from heat and release pressure using the quick release method.

4. Open the lid and add the tomatoes and squash. Close the lid again and bring to high pressure. Maintain for one minute.

5. Remove from heat and release pressure using the quick release method.

6. Open the lid, season with pepper. You may serve as toppings on rice or sandwich filler.

Midwestern Sausage Links

This tasty and savory dish is a well-known favorite of many. Make it yours, too.

Preparation Time: 5 minutes

Cooking Time: 20 minutes

Number of Servings: 4

Ingredients:

1 lb sausage links

4 potatoes, large sizes, sliced thin

1 sweet onion, diced

1 can cream of corn (16 oz)

¾ cup tomato juice

¼ teaspoon pepper

1 tablespoon oil

Salt to taste

Directions:

1. In the pressure cooker, brown sausage links over medium heat. Transfer into a platter and set aside.

2. In the cooker, arrange the following ingredients: potatoes, onion and creamed corn. Season with pepper. Put the sausage on top.

3.Pour tomato juice. Close the lid and bring to high temperature. Cook for 7 minutes.

4. Remove from heat and let the pressure subside naturally, or for about 10 minutes. Open the lid and season with salt and pepper, if needed.

5.Serve immediately.

Mushy Cornmeal Breakfast

This tasty and practical breakfast dish is a sure hit for people on the go.

Preparation Time: 5 minutes

Cooking Time: 15 minutes

Number of Servings: 6

Ingredients:

1 cup yellow cornmeal

1 tablespoon butter

4 cups water

½ teaspoon salt

Directions:

1.In a bowl, mix cornmeal in 1 cup water along with salt.

2. Pour the remaining water into the pressure cooker. Heat to boiling point. Add the cornmeal mixture and butter. Stir until it boils again.

3. Close the lid of the cooker and bring to low pressure. Cook for 10 minutes.

4.Remove from heat and remove pressure using the quick release method.

5.Open the lid, transfer to bowls and serve with cream, milk or sugar.

Cheesy Egg-Sausage Scramble
I really love this breakfast dish, so delectably cheesy and tasty!

Preparation Time: 5 minutes

Cooking Time: 15 minutes

Number of Servings: 8

Ingredients:

1 large onion, diced

3 bell peppers of different colors, diced, seeds removed

1 tablespoon oil

1 lb frozen hash browns

1 pound ground sausage

8 eggs, large sizes

½ pound grated cheddar cheese

¼ cup heavy cream

Salt and pepper to taste

Directions:

1. In the pressure cooker, add onion and bell peppers then sauté in oil for five minutes. Add sausage and hash browns.

2. Close the lid and bring to low pressure. Cook for 10 minutes,

3. Remove from heat and release pressure using the quick release method.

4. Open the lid and drain to remove excess fat, then return the cooker to medium heat.

5. In a separate bowl, mix the eggs, heavy cream, salt and pepper. Pour over the sausage mixture. Stir until the eggs begin to set.

6. Add cheese over the mixture and cook for a minute or two until the cheese melts. Serve and enjoy.

Apple and Smoked Sausage Hash Browns

Preparation Time: 5 minutes

Cooking Time: 20 minutes

Number of Servings: 4

Ingredients:

1 bag frozen hash brown potatoes, 12 ounces

2 tablespoons olive oil

2 tablespoons butter

6 ounces smoked sausage, cooked and coarsely chopped

2 medium apples, cut into thin slices

Salt and pepper to taste

Directions:

1.In the pressure cooker, add the hash brown potatoes then sauté in oil and butter. Stir occasionally for 5 minutes until they begin to brown. Add salt and pepper to taste.

2. Press potatoes firmly on the bottom of the cooker using a metal spatula, arrange sausage and apples on top of the potatoes.

3. Close the lid and bring to low pressure. Cook for 6 minutes.

4. Remove from heat and release pressure quickly.

5. Transfer to a serving dish and serve.

Hearty Quinoa Breakfast Treat

Make this breakfast treat for your family. So good and nourishing!

Preparation Time: 5 minutes

Cooking Time: 11 minutes

Number of Servings: 6

Ingredients:

2 ¼ cups water

2 tablespoons maple syrup

1 ½ cups uncooked quinoa

½ teaspoon vanilla

¼ teaspoon ground cinnamon

Salt to taste

Directions:

1.In the pressure cooker, mix together quinoa, maple syrup, water, cinnamon, vanilla and salt.

2.Close the lid and bring to low heat. Cook for 1 minute. Remove from heat and wait for 10 minutes before releasing any remaining pressure.

3.Transfer to serving bowls. Serve hot with milk, sliced almonds and berries.

Red-Eyed Country Ham

This delicious ham is made more special by gravy so tasty!

Preparation Time: 15 minutes

Cooking Time: 12 minutes

Number of Servings: 4

Ingredients:

4 pcs 4-oz slices of country ham

¾ cup coffee

1 tablespoon vegetable oil

1 teaspoon sugar

Directions:

1.In the pressure cooker, fry ham in oil, for two minutes on each side or until brown. Add coffee.

2. Close the lid of the cooker and bring to low pressure. Cook for 8 minutes.

3. Remove from heat and release pressure using the quick release method. Transfer ham to a serving platter.

4. In the mixture in the cooker, add sugar and stir until completely dissolved. Pour over the ham and serve.

Apple Oatmeal And Maple Syrup

Make your mornings special with this healthy and irresistible treat.

Preparation Time: 5 minutes

Cooking Time: 12 to 18 minutes

Number of Servings: 4

Ingredients:

½ cup dried apples, chopped

½ cup steel-cut oats

¼ cup maple syrup

¼ cup sliced almonds

¼ teaspoon salt

¼ teaspoon ground cinnamon

2 ½ cups water

Directions:

1.Mix all ingredients in the electric pressure cooker.

2.Cover the lid and bring to high temperature. Cook for 18 minutes.

3.Remove from heat and allow to normally release pressure within 10-12 minutes.

4. Open the lid and stir well. Transfer to serving bowls and enjoy!

Banana Oatmeal In Cream

A classic family favorite, so early in the morning!

Preparation Time: 5 minutes

Cooking Time: 12 to 18 minutes

Number of Servings: 4

Ingredients:

2 ripe bananas, chopped

1/2 cup steel-cut oats

1/4 cup heavy cream

1/2 teaspoon ground cinnamon

1/2 cup packed light brown sugar

2 teaspoons vanilla extract

2 ¼ cups water

Salt to taste

Directions:

1.Mix bananas, oats, vanilla, cinnamon, sugar, salt and water in the pressure cooker.

2.Close the lid and bring to high pressure. Cook for 18 minutes.

3. Remove from heat and allow pressure to be released the natural way.

4.Open the lid and stir in cream. Let stand for a minute to become warm.

5. Transfer to serving bowls and enjoy!

Walnut-Oat Porridge

This breakfast treat will give you the needed energy to keep you going all day.

Preparation Time: 5 minutes

Cooking Time: 16 to 24 minutes

Number of Servings: 6 to 8

Ingredients:

1/2 cup chopped walnuts

1/2 cup steel-cut oats

1/2 cup bulgur

1/2 teaspoon ground cinnamon

1/2 cup maple syrup

4 cups water

Salt to taste

Directions:

1.In the pressure cooker, mix all ingredients together.

2.Close the lid and bring to high pressure. Cook for 24 minutes.

3. Remove from heat and allow pressure to subside naturally.

4. Open the lid and transfer contents to a casserole. Simmer over medium heat on the stovetop for two minutes until thickened.

5. Serve immediately.

Buttered Corn Grits

Preparation Time: 8 minutes

Cooking Time: 12 to 18 minutes

Number of Servings: 4 to 6

Ingredients:

2 tablespoons unsalted butter, cut into tiny bits

1 cup of Cheddar cheese, finely grated

1 cup corn grits (not instant)

2 ½ cups water

Hot red pepper sauce to taste

Salt to taste

Directions:

1. Set the rack inside the pressure cooker and add 2 cups of water.

2. Prepare an aluminum foil sling and place a round baking dish on it.

3. In the baking dish, combine the butter, 2 ½ cups water, grits and salt then mix until smooth.

4. Use the sling to lower the baking dish into the rack of the cooker. Keep the dish uncovered. Fold the ends of the sling to fit in the cooker.

5.Close the lid and set the machine to cook at high pressure for 18 minutes.

6. Remove from heat and set aside for 5 minutes. Remove pressure using the quick release method.

7. Open the lid and remove baking dish using the foil sling.

8. Transfer to a serving dish and top with cheese and pepper sauce. Allow cheese to melt before serving.

Burritos Family Breakfast

This is something to look forward to on mornings when you are specially hungry.

Preparation Time: 8 minutes

Cooking Time: 12 to 18 minutes

Number of Servings: 4

Ingredients:

16 ounces firm tofu, drained and diced

2 tablespoons olive oil

1 cup cooked black beans, warmed

1 avocado, peeled and sliced

1/2 cup tomato, diced

1/4 cup red onion, diced

1/4 cup water

1/4 cup cilantro, chopped

1 teaspoon salt

4 large flour tortillas

Directions:

1. Fry tofu in olive oil in the pressure cooker. Sauté until brown, or for about 5 minutes. Add the tomato, onion, cilantro, water, and salt.

2. Close the lid and bring to high pressure. Cook for 6 minutes. Remove from the heat and quick-release the pressure.

3.Steam or microwave the tortillas until softened, then lay one tortilla on a flat surface to build the burrito. Place one fourth of the tofu mixture, one fourth of the drained beans, and 1/4 of the avocado slices in a line in the center of the tortilla.

4.Roll your burrito by first folding the sides of the tortilla over the filling. Then, while still holding the sides closed, fold the bottom of the tortilla over the filling. Next, roll the burrito from the bottom up, while still holding the sides closed and pushing the filling down into the burrito if it tries to spill out. Repeat for remaining burritos.

5.Top with sour cream and/or cheese, if desired.

Apple Soy Milk Oatmeal
Give your oatmeal a special touch by mixing it with your favorite dessert.

Preparation Time: 3 minutes

Cooking Time: 5 minutes

Number of Servings: 2

Ingredients:

3⁄4 cup water

1 cup milk or soymilk

1 cup quick-cooking oats

2 apples, peeled, cored, and diced

2 tablespoons brown sugar

2 teaspoons cinnamon

2 tablespoons chopped pecans

Directions:

1. Place all of the ingredients in the pressure cooker.

2. Lock the lid into place. Bring to high pressure and maintain for 5 minutes. Remove from the heat and allow pressure to release naturally.

3. Remove the lid and stir the oatmeal, adding more milk if desired.

BRUNCH

Sausage Brunch In Gravy

This dish is literally a midday delight.

Preparation Time: 5 minutes

Cooking Time: 15 minutes

Number of Servings: 8

Ingredients:

¼ cup all-purpose flour

1 pound ground pork sausage

1 green bell pepper, diced

1 red bell pepper, diced

2 cups half-and-half

Salt and pepper to taste

1 sweet onion, peeled and diced

2 tablespoons butter

Directions:

1. In the pressure cooker, fry over medium heat the sausage, onion, and bell peppers. Break apart the sausages and brown for five minutes.

2. Close the lid and bring to high pressure. Cook for 10 minutes.

3. Turn off the cooker and remove pressure using the quick release method.

4. Open the lid and add butter. Add the flour and stir continuously. Gradually pour half-and-half.

5. Bring to a boil in the stovetop, maintain for 3 minutes until gravy thickens.

6. Season to taste.

7. Serve over rice or vegetables.

Yummy Bacon-Potato Hash Browns

Late breakfast will be more exciting with this dish.

Preparation Time: 20 minutes

Cooking Time: 15 minutes

Number of Servings: 4

Ingredients:

2.2 lb potatoes, peeled

2 tablespoons parsley, finely chopped

2 tablespoons olive oil

½ lb crumbled bacon

Salt and pepper to taste

Directions:

1.Grate the potatoes or use the food processor. Rinse and place under running water for about 30 seconds. Remove moisture by using paper towels. Set aside.

2.In the pressure cooker, brown the potatoes for about 5 to 6 minutes in olive oil. Season with salt and pepper.

3.Add parsley and bacon and mix well. Press the mixture firmly onto the bottom of the cooker.

4. Close the lid and bring to high pressure. Cook for 6 to 7 minutes.

5. Turn off the cooker and release pressure using the quick release method.

6. Open the lid and transfer the hash browns into a serving plate.

7. Serve hot with coffee or juice.

Delightful Egg Muffins

With this delicious muffin, you would wish that every mealtime is brunch.

Preparation Time: 10 minutes

Cooking Time: 8 minutes

Number of Servings: 4

Ingredients:

4 eggs

1/4 teaspoon lemon pepper seasoning

4 tablespoons cheddar cheese, shredded

1 green onion, diced

4 slices bacon, precooked and crumbled

Directions:

1. Prepare the pressure cooker by placing the steamer basket and adding 1 ½ cups water.

2. In a large measuring dish, break the eggs and add lemon pepper. Beat well.

3. Place four muffin cups on a platter. Add cheese, bacon and onion equally among the cups. Pour the egg mixture into the muffin cups. Stir with a fork to mix.

4. Put the cups in the steamer basket and close the lid. Bring to high temperature and cook for 8 minutes.

5. Turn off the cooker and wait for 2 minutes before releasing the pressure using the quick release method.

6. Open the lid, and carefully remove the muffin cups.

7. Serve immediately.

Chicken And Lentils Salad

Serve this dish on lettuce cups for brunch.

Preparation Time: 10 minutes

Cooking Time: 8 minutes

Number of Servings: 6

Ingredients:

2 small apples, peeled and diced, divided

1 cup seedless grapes, cut in half

1 cup dried lentils

1 teaspoon lemon juice

½ cup cashews, roasted

1 teaspoon olive oil

2 stalks celery, diced

1½ pounds chicken breasts, boneless and skinless

2 cups water

2½ teaspoons curry powder, divided

¾ cup plain yogurt or sour cream

¼ cup mayonnaise

½ small red onion, peeled and diced

6 cups mixed green salad

Directions:

1. Mix the apples with the lemon juice to prevent browning. Bring the oil to temperature in the pressure cooker over medium-high heat.

2. Cut the chicken into bite-sized pieces; add to the pressure cooker and stir-fry for 5 minutes or until browned. Stir in the lentils, water, and 1 teaspoon of the curry powder. Add half the apples.

2. Close the lid and bring the pressure cooker to low pressure; maintain pressure for 8 minutes.

3.Remove from the heat and allow pressure to release naturally.

4. Transfer the contents of the pressure cooker to a bowl. Once it's cooled, stir in the remaining diced apple, grapes, cashews, celery, and red onion.

5. To make the dressing, mix together the yogurt or sour cream, mayonnaise, and remaining 1½ teaspoons curry powder.

5. For each serving, place 1 cup of the salad greens on a plate. Add the lentil mixture on top of the lettuce and drizzle with the dressing.

6.For a sweeter taste, add a pinch or two of sugar to the dressing, if desired.

Scrambled Tofu Gourmet

Serve this delicious dish for a heartwarming meal.

Preparation Time: 10 minutes

Cooking Time: 12 minutes

Number of Servings: 4

Ingredients:

16 ounces firm tofu, drained and mashed

1 teaspoon fresh lemon juice

1 tablespoon olive oil

1/2 cup tomato, diced

2 tablespoons parsley, chopped

1/2 teaspoon black pepper

1/2 teaspoon turmeric

1 clove garlic, minced

1/2 cup button mushrooms, sliced

1/2 cup broccoli florets, blanched

1/4 cup water

1 teaspoon salt

Directions:

1. In a large bowl, mash the tofu with your hands or a fork, then stir in the lemon juice, salt, pepper, and turmeric. Set aside.

2. Bring the olive oil to medium heat in the pressure cooker. Add the broccoli and mushrooms and sauté for 5 minutes. Add the tomato and garlic, and sauté for an additional 30 seconds.

3. Pour in the tofu mixture and water and stir.

4. Close the lid and bring to medium pressure. Cook for 6 minutes.

5. Remove from heat and release the pressure using the natural method.

6. Open the lid and add parsley. Serve hot.

Tofu With Vegetables Medley

Sometimes what we need is to have something that will make us really satisfied, and this dish proves to be one.

Preparation Time: 10 minutes

Cooking Time: 5 minutes

Number of Servings: 4

Ingredients:

1 16-ounce package extra-firm tofu

1 cup broccoli, blanched and chopped

2 tablespoons vegetable oil

2 tablespoons soy sauce

1/2 onion, diced

1/2 zucchini, chopped

1/2 cup yellow squash, chopped

1/2 green bell pepper, chopped

1 cup water

1/4 cup nutritional yeast

Directions:

1. Wrap the block of tofu in paper towels and press for 5 minutes by adding weight on top. Remove the paper towels and cut the tofu into 1/2"-thick pieces. Add 1 tablespoon of oil to the pressure cooker and sauté the tofu until it is light brown on all sides. Add 1 tablespoon of soy sauce and sauté for 10 seconds more. Remove the tofu.

2. Place the water in the pressure cooker along with the steamer tray. Place the tofu on top of the steamer tray. Lock the lid into place; bring to high pressure and maintain for 5 minutes. Remove from the heat and allow pressure to release naturally.

3. Add 1 tablespoon of oil to a large pan and sauté the onion, broccoli, bell pepper, zucchini, and squash until tender. Add the tofu and 1 tablespoon soy sauce and sauté for 1 minute more. Sprinkle the nutritional yeast on top and serve.

Hearty Mexican Tofu

Get a dose of Mexican taste with this tofu experience.

Preparation Time: 15 minutes

Cooking Time: 20 minutes

Number of Servings: 4

Ingredients:

16 ounces firm tofu, drained and mashed

8 corn tortillas

2 tablespoons olive oil

1 teaspoon fresh lemon juice

1 teaspoon salt

1 cup vegetarian refried beans, warmed

1/2 cup cheese or vegan cheese

1/4 cup onion, diced

1/2 teaspoon turmeric

1/2 teaspoon black pepper

1 clove garlic, minced

1/2 cup chipotle salsa

Directions:

1. Preheat the oven to 350°F. In a large bowl, mash the tofu with your hands or a fork, then stir in the lemon juice, salt, pepper, and turmeric.

2. Bring 1 tablespoon olive oil to medium heat in the pressure cooker. Add the onion and sauté for 3 minutes. Add the garlic and sauté for an additional 30 seconds.

101

3. Pour in the tofu mixture and stir, then lock the lid into place. Bring to medium pressure and maintain for 6 minutes. Remove from the heat and allow pressure to release naturally.

4. Heat 1 tablespoon olive oil in a small sauté pan over medium heat. Cook the tortillas one at a time, until they begin to brown on each side.

5. Place all eight of the tortillas on one or two baking sheets. Divide the refried beans evenly among the tortillas, then top with the cooked tofu mixture. Sprinkle cheese over each of the tortillas, then bake until the cheese begins to melt.

6. Remove from the oven and top with salsa before serving.

Mid-Morning Diced Fries

Make your fries more delectable by serving with a variety of dips and toppings.

Preparation Time: 15 minutes

Cooking Time: 20 minutes

Number of Servings: 4

Ingredients:

4 cups red potatoes, diced

2 tablespoons olive oil

1 teaspoon chili powder

1 1/2 teaspoons paprika

1 teaspoon black pepper

1 1/2 teaspoons salt

Directions:

1. In the pressure cooker, sauté potatoes in olive oil for 3 minutes.

2. Add the remaining ingredients and mix well.

3. Close the lid and bring to high temperature. Cook for 7 minutes.

4. Remove from heat and release the pressure using quick release method.

5. Serve with ketchup or mayonnaise. Enjoy!

Chicken Alfredo Pasta And Mushrooms

I really love pasta with white sauces, especially this one. Yummy!

Preparation Time: 15 minutes

Cooking Time: 20 minutes

Number of Servings: 6

Ingredients:

2 tablespoons olive oil

8 ounces fresh mushrooms, cleaned and sliced

1½ pounds boneless, skinless chicken breasts

1/2 onion, diced

1 red bell pepper, seeded and diced

8 ounces sugar snap peas, sliced diagonally

1½ cups cauliflower segments

1½ cups broccoli florets

½ cup sliced carrots

1 (14-ounce) can chicken broth

1 onion, peeled and diced

1 tablespoon dried basil

4 cloves garlic, peeled and minced

1/8 teaspoon freshly ground nutmeg

1 teaspoon dried thyme

¼ teaspoon freshly ground black pepper

¼ cup Parmesan cheese, grated

1 stick butter, softened

1 cup whole milk

8 ounces uncooked linguini

Directions:

1. Add oil to the pressure cooker on medium heat. Cut the chicken into bite-sized pieces and add to the pressure cooker; stir-fry for 5 minutes or until they begin to brown. Add the onion and red bell pepper; sauté for 3 minutes. Add the sliced mushrooms; sauté for 3 minutes. Add the basil, garlic, nutmeg, thyme, pepper, and the broth. Stir to combine. Lock the lid then bring to low pressure; maintaining pressure for 3 minutes. Remove from the heat and quick-release the pressure. Remove the lid.

2. Add the sugar snap peas, carrots, broccoli, and cauliflower to the pressure cooker. Return the pressure cooker to the heat, lock the lid, and bring to low pressure; maintain 3 minutes. Remove from the heat and quick-release the pressure.

3. Whip the cheese into the butter and then blend with the milk. Return the pressure cooker to medium heat. Stir in the cream mixture; cook and stir for 3 minutes.

4. Cook the linguini according to package directions. Top the noodles with the sauce and additional grated cheese if desired.

Fettuccine In Smoked Salmon Sauce

This is great way to eat pasta with wonderfully tasty smoked salmon sauce.

Preparation Time: 15 minutes

Cooking Time: 20 minutes

Number of Servings: 6

Ingredients:

¼ cup olive oil

2 cups fettuccine

4 cups chicken broth

½ teaspoon sea salt

¼ teaspoon freshly ground white pepper

1 teaspoon dried thyme

3 tablespoons butter

½ cup sour cream

2 green onions, cleaned and diced

1 pound smoked salmon, in bite-sized pieces

1/3 cup Parmesan cheese, grated

Directions:

1. Bring the oil to temperature in the pressure cooker over medium heat. Stir in the fettuccine, broth, salt, pepper, and thyme. Lock the lid in place and bring to high pressure; maintain pressure for 8 minutes. Quick-release the pressure and remove the lid.

2. Drain the pasta if necessary. Transfer to a serving bowl. Cut the butter into small chunks and toss with the pasta. Add the sour cream; stir to combine. Add the green onion and smoked salmon; toss to mix. Top with the grated cheese. Serve.

Mama's Vegetable Casserole

Once you cook this once, you'll always want to cook it over and over again.

Preparation Time: 15 minutes

Cooking Time: 8 minutes

Number of Servings: 4

Ingredients:

2 tablespoons vegetable oil

1 onion, diced

1/2 green bell pepper, chopped

1 8-ounce package sausages

3 cups potatoes, peeled and shredded

6 eggs, beaten, or 16 ounces firm crumbled tofu

1 cup cottage cheese

2 cups Cheddar cheese

Salt and pepper, to taste

Directions:

1. Add the vegetable oil to the pressure cooker and sauté the onion and bell pepper until tender. Add the crumbles and cook for 2–3 minutes more. Add the rest of the ingredients to the pressure cooker.

2. Lock the lid into place; bring to high pressure and maintain for 5 minutes. Remove from the heat and allow pressure to release naturally.

3. Transfer to serving plates and serve.

APPETIZERS

Yoghurt Cream With Asparagus
This dish is appetizingly wonderful!

Preparation Time: 4 hours

Cooking Time: 5 minutes

Number of Servings: 4

Ingredients:

1 pound asparagus, trimmed

2 cups plain whole yogurt

1 1/4 teaspoons salt

1 cup water

Directions:

1. Make the yogurt crème by putting the yogurt in a fine mesh strainer over a bowl and putting it in the refrigerator for about 4 hours or until it has reached the consistency of sour cream.

2. Place water in the pressure cooker and add the steamer basket.

3. Lay asparagus flat in steamer basket. If it does not fit in one layer, make a second layer perpendicular to the first. Sprinkle with salt. Close and lock the lid.

4. Turn the heat up to high and when the cooker reaches pressure, lower to the minimum needed to maintain pressure. Cook for 2–3 minutes at high pressure.

5. When time is up, open the pressure cooker by releasing pressure.

6. Serve with yogurt crème.

Tasty Garlic Spread

Preparation Time: 4 hours

Cooking Time: 5 minutes

Number of Servings: 10 spoonfuls

Ingredients:

2 whole heads garlic

2 tablespoons fresh basil

1 cup water

1/2 cup butter, softened

2 tablespoons fresh oregano

1/2 teaspoon salt

Directions:

1. Cut the tops off of each head of garlic.

2. Pour water into the pressure cooker, then add the steamer basket. Add the garlic.

3. Lock the lid into place; bring to high pressure and maintain for 2 minutes. Remove from the heat and allow pressure to quick-release.

4. Once the garlic has cooled, peel away the paper until you are left with only the cloves.

5. In a small bowl, mash the cloves then add the butter, basil, oregano, and salt. Refrigerate for 1 hour before serving.

Yummy Chicken Roulades

This is a healthy and satisfying dish that I really like.

Preparation Time: 30 minutes

Cooking Time: 12 minutes

Number of Servings: 32

Ingredients:

4 boneless, skinless chicken breast halves

12 large fresh spinach leaves plus additional fresh spinach leaves for garnish, divided

2/3 cup garden vegetable-flavored cream cheese or cream cheese, softened

1/2 teaspoon dried basil leaves

1 jar (7.25 ounces) roasted red peppers, drained

1/4 teaspoon pepper

1/2 cup chicken broth or water

1/2 teaspoon salt

Directions:

1. Bat out the chicken by placing it between plastic wrap sheets.

2. Season the chicken, and cover with cream cheese, dust with basil.

3. Lay 3 spinach leaves and red peppers on the chicken.

4. Roll up each chicken piece and hold together with a cocktail stick.

5. Put the meat rack in the cooker and add the broth or water.

6. Place the chicken in seam side down.

7. Place the lid on and cook for 12 mins.

8. Cool down using quick release.

9. Take out the chicken and remove the sticks, slice into 8 pieces.

10. Makes 32 appetizers.

Pressurized Sloppy Joe

Try this once and you'll be hooked.

Preparation Time: 30 minutes

Cooking Time: 12 minutes

Number of Servings: 6

Ingredients:

11/2 pounds lean ground beef or ground turkey

1 large sweet onion, peeled and diced

2 cloves garlic, peeled and minced

1/2 cup beef broth

1/4 cup tomato paste

1 tablespoon olive oil

2 tablespoons light brown sugar

Salt and freshly ground black pepper, to taste

1/2 teaspoon chili powder

1 tablespoon Worcestershire sauce

1 teaspoon prepared mustard

Pinch ground cloves

Pinch dried red pepper flakes

Directions:

1. Bring the oil to temperature in the pressure cooker over medium-high heat. Add the onion and sauté for 3 minutes. Add the garlic; sauté for 30 seconds.

2. Stir in the remaining ingredients. Lock the lid into place and bring to low pressure; maintain pressure for 10 minutes.

3. Quick-release the pressure and, leaving the pan over the heat, remove the lid. Remove and discard any fat floating on top of the meat mixture.

4. Stir and simmer, breaking apart the cooked ground meat to thicken the sauce. Serve by spooning onto hamburger buns.

Green Peppers With Beef Stuffing
I always look for this dish during parties and wonder why it tastes so great.

Preparation Time: 30 minutes

Cooking Time: 15 to 20 minutes

Number of Servings: 4

Ingredients:

1 pound lean ground beef

4 medium green bell peppers

1 cup cooked rice

3 cloves garlic, peeled and minced

2 large eggs

1 small yellow onion, peeled and diced

Salt and freshly ground black pepper, to taste

1/2 cup chicken broth

111

1/2 cup tomato sauce

Directions:

1. Cut the tops off the green peppers. Remove and discard the seeds and use a spoon to scrape out and discard some of the white pith inside the peppers. Set aside.

2. Dice any of the green pepper that you can salvage from around the stem and mix well with ground beef, rice, eggs, garlic, onion, salt and pepper.

3. Evenly divide the meat mixture between the green peppers. Place the rack in the pressure cooker and pour the broth into the cooker.

4. Place the peppers on the rack and pour the tomato sauce over the peppers. Lock the lid into place and bring to low pressure; maintain pressure for 15 minutes.

5. Quick-release the pressure. Remove the peppers to serving plates. Remove the rack and pour the pan juices into a gravy boat to pass at the table.

Heart Stuffed Potato Skins

Take a bite of this very popular appetizer. Now.

Preparation Time: 30 minutes

Cooking Time: 15 to 20 minutes

Number of Servings: 6

Ingredients:

6 Idaho potatoes

2 cups water

1 tablespoon vegetable oil

8 ounces shredded Cheddar cheese

1/8 cup soy bacon bits

4 tablespoons thinly sliced scallions

1/4 cup sour cream

Directions:

1. Preheat the oven to 400°F.

2. Wash the potatoes, then slice each in half lengthwise. Pour water into the pressure cooker. Add the steamer basket and arrange the potatoes in one or two layers.

3. Lock the lid into place. Bring to high pressure; maintain pressure for 10 minutes. Quick-release the pressure, then remove the lid.

4. Remove the potatoes from the pressure cooker and scoop out the inside, leaving a 1/4-thick shell.

5. Brush the scooped-out shell of each potato with oil and arrange on an ungreased baking sheet.

6. Cook the potato skins for 15 minutes, or until the edges begin to brown, then remove from the oven.

7. Fill the potato skins with the cheese and bake for an additional 5 to 10 minutes, or until the cheese has melted.

8. Top each skin with soy bacon bits, sliced scallions, and a dollop of sour cream.

Pressure Cooked Black Beans Dip
Perfect for dipping tortillas, corn chips or tacos.

Preparation Time: 10 minutes

Cooking Time: 22 minutes

Number of Servings: 12

Ingredients:

1 cup dried black beans

2 cups water

1 tablespoon olive oil

1 small onion, peeled and diced

3 cloves garlic, peeled and minced

1 14.5-ounce can diced tomatoes

2 4-ounce cans mild green chilies, finely chopped

1 teaspoon chili powder

1/2 teaspoon dried oregano

1/4 cup fresh cilantro, finely chopped

Salt, to taste

1 cup cheese, grated

Directions:

1. Add the beans and water to a container; cover and let the beans soak 8 hours at room temperature.

2. Add the oil and the onions to the pressure cooker; sauté for 3 minutes or until the onion is soft. Add the garlic and sauté for 30 seconds.

3. Drain the beans and add them to the pressure cooker along with the tomatoes, chilies, chili powder, and oregano. Stir well. Lock the lid into place. Bring to high pressure; maintain pressure for 12 minutes. Remove from heat and allow pressure to release naturally for 10 minutes.

4. Quick-release any remaining pressure. Remove the lid. Transfer the cooked beans mixture to a food processor or blender. Add the cilantro and process until smooth. Taste for seasoning; add salt if desired.

5. Transfer the dip to a bowl. Stir in the cheese. Serve warm.

Pearl Onions With Sweet And Sour Sauce

Bite into the onion's succulence and tell me you want more.

Preparation Time: 30 minutes

Cooking Time: 15 to 20 minutes

Number of Servings: 6

Ingredients:

1 pound pearl onions, outer layer removed

1/2 cup water

1/8 teaspoon salt

1 bay leaf

4 tablespoons balsamic vinegar

1 tablespoon honey

1 tablespoon flour

Directions:

1. Put the onions in the pressure cooker with water, salt, and the bay leaf. Close and lock the lid.

2. Turn the heat up to high and when the cooker reaches pressure, lower to the minimum needed to maintain pressure. Cook for 5–6 minutes at low pressure (3 minutes at high pressure).

3. While the onions are cooking, combine the vinegar, honey, and flour in a small saucepan. Stir over low heat until well combined (about 30 seconds).

4. When time is up, open the pressure cooker by releasing pressure.

5. Pour the balsamic vinegar mixture over the onions and mix well. Remove bay leaf.

6. Transfer to serving dish and serve, or let sit overnight in refrigerator prior to serving.

Parsley-Chickpea-Dill Dip

This versatile dip may be used on almost any finger food.

Preparation Time: 30 minutes

Cooking Time: 20 minutes

Number of Servings: 20 spoonfuls

Ingredients:

1 cup dried chickpeas

8 cups water

3 tablespoons olive oil

1/8 cup fresh dill

1/8 cup fresh parsley

2 cloves garlic, minced

1 tablespoon fresh lemon juice

2 tablespoons water

3/4 teaspoon salt

Directions:

1. Add the chickpeas and 4 cups water to the pressure cooker. Lock the lid into place; bring to high pressure for 1 minute. Remove from the heat and quick-release the pressure.

2. Drain the water, rinse the chickpeas, and add to the pressure cooker again with the remaining 4 cups of water. Let soak for 1 hour.

3. Add 1 tablespoon olive oil. Lock the lid into place; bring to high pressure and maintain for 20 minutes. Remove from the heat and allow pressure to release naturally. Drain chickpeas and water.

4. Add the drained chickpeas, dill, parsley, garlic, lemon juice, and water to a blender or food processor. Blend for just 30 seconds.

5. With the food processor lid still in place, gradually add the remaining oil while still blending, and also add the salt.

Spicy And Cheesy Jalapeno Dip
For added spice, try this for your dips.

Preparation Time: 30 minutes

Cooking Time: 20 minutes

Number of Servings: 12

Ingredients:

2 tablespoons butter, or vegan margarine

2 tablespoons flour

1 cup milk, or unsweetened vegan soymilk

8 ounces shredded Cheddar cheese

1/2 cup canned tomatoes

1/2 cup pickled jalapeños

2 tablespoons lemon juice

Salt and pepper, to taste

Directions:

1. In the pressure cooker, soften butter over medium-high heat and gradually add flour until you have a paste. Add milk and stir until it has thickened and there are no lumps. Bring the mixture to a boil.

2. Add the cheese and stir until smooth. Add the tomatoes and jalapeños and secure the lid on the pressure cooker. Cook on medium until the pressure-indicator rises. Lower heat and cook for 3 minutes.

3. Allow the pressure to release and remove the lid. Add the lemon juice, salt, and pepper.

Easy Taco Chips Dip

Tacos never tasted this good when dipped in this!

Preparation Time: 30 minutes

Cooking Time: 25 minutes

Number of Servings: 12

Ingredients:

1 pound ground beef or turkey

1 cup dried kidney beans

1 large onion, peeled and diced

2 cups water

1/4 cup olive oil

2 cloves garlic, peeled and minced

2 teaspoons chili powder

1 8-ounce can tomato sauce

1 cup beef broth

1 tablespoon light brown sugar

1 teaspoon ground cumin

Salt, to taste

Directions:

1. Put the beans and water in a covered container and let soak at room temperature overnight. When ready to prepare the dip, drain the beans.

2. Bring the olive oil to temperature in the pressure cooker. Add the onion and sauté for 3 minutes or until softened. Add the ground beef or turkey; stir and break apart until the meat is no longer pink. Drain off any fat rendered from the meat. Add the garlic and stir into the meat.

3. Add the beans, tomato sauce, broth, brown sugar, chili powder and cumin. Stir well.

4. Lock the lid into place and bring to high pressure; maintain pressure for 10 minutes. Remove from the heat and allow pressure to release naturally for 10 minutes. Quick-release any remaining pressure and remove the lid. Stir the dip, crushing the beans into the mixture. For a smooth dip, use an immersion blender or transfer the dip to a food processor or blender and process. Taste for seasoning and add salt if needed. Serve warm.

Tender Steamy Artichokes
If you love artichokes, you will enjoy the delightful taste of this recipe.

Preparation Time: 5 minutes

Cooking Time: 10 minutes

Number of Servings: 6

Ingredients:

6 artichokes

1 cup water

Juice of 1 lemon

Directions:

1. Clean the artichokes by cutting off the top one-third and removing the tough exterior leaves.

2. Place artichokes upright in the steamer basket.

3. Fill the pressure cooker base with water and lemon juice, and then lower the steamer basket into the cooker. Close and lock the lid.

4. The cooking time will depend on the size of the artichokes. A large globe artichoke that almost fills the pressure cooker could take 10 minutes, while medium artichokes only need about 5 minutes.

5. Turn the heat up to high and when the cooker reaches pressure, lower to the minimum needed to maintain pressure. Cook for 5–10 minutes at high pressure.

6. When time is up, open the pressure cooker by releasing pressure.

7. Lift very carefully out of the pressure cooker and serve.

Simple Carrot Coins

Tasty, yummy nutritious vegetable.

Preparation Time: 10 minutes

Cooking Time: 5 minutes

Number of Servings: 6

Ingredients:

1 pound thick carrots, peeled and sliced into 1/4-inch thick coins

1 cup water

Directions:

1. Fill the pressure cooker base with water. Fill the steamer basket with carrot coins and lower the basket into the cooker. Close and lock the lid.

2. Turn the heat up to high and when the cooker reaches pressure, lower to the minimum needed to maintain pressure. Cook 3–4 minutes at low pressure (1–2 minutes at high pressure).

3. When time is up, open the pressure cooker by releasing pressure.

4. Pour into serving dish immediately to stop the cooking.

Pressurized Boiled Peanuts
A favorite of the young and old alike.

Preparation Time: 5 minutes

Cooking Time: 45 minutes

Number of Servings: 16

Ingredients:

2 pounds raw peanuts

12 cups water

1/3 cup salt

Directions:

1. Rinse the peanuts under cold water then place in the pressure cooker. Add the water and salt.

2. Lock the lid in place; bring to 10 pounds of pressure, or a medium setting, and cook for 45 minutes. Remove from the heat and allow pressure to release naturally.

3. Let the peanuts cool in the water, then drain.

DESSERTS

Walnut Fudge Candies
Loosen up and enjoy this delightful chocolate dessert!

Preparation Time: 20 minutes

Cooking Time: 5 minutes

Number of Servings: makes 50 candies

Ingredients:

12 oz. semi-sweet chocolate chips

14 oz. sweetened condensed milk

1 cup walnuts, chopped

1 teaspoon vanilla

2 cups water

Directions:

1. In a stainless steel bowl, mix milk and chocolate chips and cover with aluminum foil.

2. Place water, cooking rack, and the steel bowl in the pressure cooker. Close lid and bring to high pressure. Cook for five minutes.

3. Turn off the cooker and release pressure using the quick release method.

4. Open the lid and remove the bowl. Add nuts and vanilla. Mix until well-blended.

5. Spoon the mixture onto waxed paper or paper candy cups. Cool before serving.

Decadent Fruit-Glazed Cheesecake

Delight yourself by dipping into this smooth and yummy decadent cheesecake.

Preparation Time: 20 minutes

Cooking Time: 5 minutes

Number of Servings: makes 50 candies

Ingredients:

16 oz. cream cheese

¼ cup heavy cream

¾ cup sugar

4 tablespoons bread crumbs

1 tablespoon butter

2 teaspoons vanilla

2 tablespoons flour

6 tablespoons sour cream

2 teaspoons grated lemon zest

2 whole eggs

2 egg yolks

2 cups water

Directions:

1. Apply butter all over the sides of a baking dish or springform pan. Scatter bread crumbs evenly all over the pan. Set aside.

2. In a bowl, mix the cream cheese, sugar, vanilla, cream, flour, sour cream, and lemon zest. Add in eggs and egg yolks. Mix well and pour into the baking dish.

3. Cover the top of the dish with an aluminum foil. Place the trivet in the pressure cooker and add water. Place the foil-covered pan in the center of the trivet.

4. Close the lid of the cooker and bring to high pressure. Cook for 30 minutes. Turn off the cooker and release pressure naturally.

5. Open the lid and remove the pan using tongs. Chill for 4 hours or more.

6. Before serving, decorate with fruit toppings or fruit preserves over the cheesecake layer.

Buttery Rice Pudding

An all-time favorite dessert.

Preparation Time: 20 minutes

Cooking Time: 15 to 20 minutes

Number of Servings: 4

Ingredients:

¼ cup long grain rice

1 tablespoon butter

2 cups milk

1 cup water

1/3 cup sugar

¼ cup evaporated milk

½ teaspoon vanilla

1 egg

Cinnamon to taste

Salt to taste

Directions:

1. In the pressure cooker, melt butter and add rice. Mix thoroughly. Pour water and fresh milk, then stir in sugar and salt.

2. Close the lid of the cooker and bring to pressure. Cook for 12 minutes.

3. Turn off the cooker and allow pressure to be released using the natural method.

4. Open the lid and set aside.

5. In another bowl, mix egg, milk and vanilla. Add to the mixture in the pressure cooker. Cook over medium heat and stir continuously until mixture begins to bubble.

6. Turn off the cooker and cool for 10 minutes while stirring occasionally.

7. Place in dessert dishes and refrigerate before serving with cinnamon sprinkles.

Pressurized Cheesecake

Cheesecake is one of my comfort foods. Deliciously tasty!

Preparation Time: 1 hour and 10 minutes

Cooking Time: 25 to 30 minutes

Number of Servings: 6

Ingredients:

Crust:

1/2 cup chocolate graham cracker cookies, crushed

2 tablespoons butter, melted

Filling:

12-ounces cream cheese

1 tablespoon all-purpose flour

1/2 cup sugar

1/4 cup sour cream

1/4 cup heavy cream

1 1/2 teaspoons vanilla extract

1 egg yolk

2 eggs

Topping:

1 1/2 cups sweetened shredded coconut

12 chewy caramels, unwrapped

3 tablespoons heavy cream

Directions:

1. Coat a 7 inch springform pan with non-stick spray.

2. Combine graham cracker crumbs and butter in a small bowl. Use this mixture to cover the bottom and sides of the pan. Freeze for 10 minutes.

3. Using a hand mixer, mix cream cheese and sugar at medium speed, followed by heavy cream, sour cream, flour, vanilla and eggs. Do not overmix. Pour on top of the crust and cover with aluminum foil.

4. Pour 2 cups of water in the pressure cooker. Place trivet and put on top of it the filled pan. Use a foil sling in lowering to the pressure cooking pot. Fold the sling so it won't get in the way when closing the lid.

5. Close the lid and bring to high pressure. Cook for 35 minutes.

6. Turn off the cooker and allow pressure to be released naturally or for 10 minutes.

126

7. Open the lid and check to see if cheesecake is done. If not, cook for additional 5 minutes.

8. Remove the pan and let cool. Remove foil and cover with plastic wrap. Refrigerate for 4 hours or more.

9. After chilling, add toppings.

10. To prepare toppings, toast in an oven the shredded coconut until golden brown. Let cool.

11. Put caramels and cream in a microwaveable bowl. Cook in microwave for 1 to 2 minutes. Stir every 20 seconds. Add the toasted coconut and stir well.

12. Spread the toppings on top of the cheesecake.

13. Slice and serve.

Crispy Sliced Apple

For apple fans out there, this one's for you!

Preparation Time: 20 minutes

Cooking Time: 15 minutes

Number of Servings: 6

Ingredients:

4 apples, cored, peeled & sliced thin

1/2 cup old-fashioned oats

1/4 cup brown sugar, packed light

1 1/3 tbsp. lemon juice

1 cup warm water

4 tbsp. butter

1/4 cup flour

Salt to taste

2 tsp. ground cinnamon

Directions:

1. Sprinkle apples with lemon juice in a bowl. In a separate bowl, mix flour, oats, sugar, cinnamon, butter and salt.

2. In a 6-inch baking dish, layer the following alternatively: apples and oat mixture. Finish with oat mixture on top. Cover dish with foil.

3. Pour 1 cup of warm water in the pressure cooker. Place the covered dish on rack inside the cooker.

4. Close the lid and bring to high temperature. Cook for 15 minutes.

5. Turn off the cooker and allow pressure to be released naturally. Open the lid and remove the baking dish from the cooker. Remove cover and let cool.

6. Serve.

Pressurized Crème Brulee
Easy to prepare, yet delightfully good!

Preparation Time: 10 minutes

Cooking Time: 4 minutes

Number of Servings: 4

Ingredients:

2 cups warm heavy cream

1 tsp. vanilla extract

4 egg yolks, large

3/4 cup sugar

3 teaspoons sugar

1 cup warm water

Directions:

1. Except for the 3 teaspoons sugar and warm water, mix all ingredients together. Transfer to 4 4-oz baking dishes. Wrap each dish with foil.

2. Pour 1 cup of warm water in the pressure cooker. Place the foil-wrapped dishes in the cooker.

3. Close the lid and bring to medium temperature. Cook for 4 minutes.

4. Turn off the cooker and release pressure using the natural method.

5. Open the lid and carefully remove the wrapped dishes. Refrigerate for 3 hours.

6. Remove cover, sprinkle sugar on top and place under the broiler to caramelize.

7. Serve.

Chocolatey Custard Delight
Mouth-watering and simply delectable way to complete a meal.

Preparation Time: 25 minutes

Cooking Time: 30 minutes

Number of Servings: 6 to 8

Ingredients:

1 lb dark cooking chocolate, finely chopped

8 oz full cream milk

8 oz cream

6 egg yolks

½ cup sugar

1 teaspoon vanilla extract

Directions:

1. In a bowl, mix milk, cream, sugar and vanilla. Heat until just about to simmer.

2. Remove from heat and add chocolate pieces. Mix well until melted.

3. Beat egg yolks and slowly add to the chocolate mixture.

4. Pour into round baking dish and place in the pressure cooker with trivet and 4 cups water underneath.

5. Close the lid and bring to high pressure. Cook for 30 minutes.

6. Turn off the cooker and carefully remove the dish.

7. Top with fruits if desired. Serve.

All-Star French Pudding

Preparation Time: 25 minutes

Cooking Time: 30 minutes

Number of Servings: 6

Ingredients:

4 slices day-old French bread, cut in cubes

1 tablespoon butter

1/2 cup chopped walnuts

1/2 cup packed light brown sugar

1/2 teaspoon cinnamon

3 cups water

1/2 cup golden raisins

Zest of 1/2 orange, in very thin strips

1/2 teaspoon vanilla

1/4 teaspoon salt

2 eggs, lightly beaten

2 cups warm milk

Cinnamon

Directions:

1. Spread butter on a 6-cup baking dish, set aside.

2. In another bowl, combine raisins, walnuts, orange zest and bread. Set aside.

3. Yet in another bowl, mix brown sugar, cinnamon, milk, eggs, vanilla and salt. Pour over the milk mixture and transfer to the buttered baking dish. Cover tightly with foil. Pour water into the cooker and place the pudding mix into the center of it.

4. Close the lid and bring to pressure. Cook for 20 minutes.

5. Turn off the cooker and allow pressure to be released using the natural release method.

6. Open the lid and remove the baking dish. Let cool.

7. Serve with cinnamon sprinkled on top.

Cinnamon Fruit Medley

Delicious mix of dried fruits combined with tasty cinnamon.

Preparation Time: 25 minutes

Cooking Time: 30 minutes

Number of Servings: 6

Ingredients:

1 lb mixed dried fruits or raisins

3/4 cup packed brown sugar

2 lemon slices

1 cup red wine

1 cup water

1 cinnamon stick

Directions:

1. In the pressure cooker, add together wine, water, lemon slices, sugar, and cinnamon stick. Bring to a boil and simmer.

2. Add the dried fruits.

3. Cover the lid and bring to high pressure. Cook for 5 minutes.

4. Turn off the cooker and remove pressure using quick release method.

5. Open the lid and transfer contents to a serving dish.

6. Serve warm with whipped cream, if desired.

Quickie Hazelnut Flan

This reminds me of my grandmother who cooks it with love and affection.

Preparation Time: 25 minutes

Cooking Time: 15 minutes

Number of Servings: 8

Ingredients:

For the Caramel:

1/4 cup water

3/4 cup granulated sugar

For the Custard:

2 egg yolks

3 whole eggs

2 tablespoons Hazelnut syrup

1/2 cup whipping cream

2 cups whole milk

1/3 cup granulated sugar

1 teaspoon vanilla extract

Salt to taste

Directions:

1. To prepare caramel, Bring to boil the water and sugar. Do not stir. Cook until mixture is brown.

2. Remove from heat and pour into 8 custard cups, tilting gently to cover the bottom. Set aside.

3. In another mixing bowl, beat egg yolks, 1/3 cup sugar and a pinch of salt. Set aside.

4. Heat milk in a saucepan until bubble appears. Remove from heat and add to the egg mixture. Add cream, vanilla and hazelnut syrup. Strain the mixture into another mixing bowl.

5. Place trivet at the bottom of the pressure cooker and add water.

6. Pour the mixture into the custard cups. Cover with aluminum foil and place over the trivet in the pressure cooker.

7. Close the lid and bring to high pressure. Cook for 6 minutes on high pressure. Turn off the cooker and release pressure using the quick release method.

8. Open the lid and remove the cups. Uncover each cup and let cool naturally. Refrigerate for at least 4 hours or overnight.

9. Flip the custard cup on a serving dish before serving. Enjoy!

Elegant Pears In Raspberry Sauce

Enjoy this chic dessert can with your loved ones.

Preparation Time: 25 minutes

Cooking Time: 30 minutes

Number of Servings: 6

Ingredients:

4 pears, peeled, stems on

3/4 cup red wine 2 cups water

4 tablespoons heavy cream

1/2 cup sugar

1 cup frozen raspberries

2 slices lemon

2 cinnamon sticks

1/4 teaspoon mace

Directions:

1.Combine water, lemon, cinnamon sticks, sugar and mace in the pressure cooker. Stir until sugar is dissolved.

2. Put the pears in the steamer basket and make sure they stand upright. Place the basket into the pressure cooker.

3. Close the lid and bring to high pressure. Cook for 2 minutes.

4. Turn off the cooker and release the pressure using the quick release method.

5. Remove the lid and add the red wine.

6. Close the lid and bring to high pressure again for another 2 minutes.

7. Turn off the cooker and release the pressure using the quick release method.

8. Remove the lid. Lift the steamer basket and transfer the pears to another container. Boil the remaining liquid in the cooker until it becomes syrupy. Let cool and coat the pears with it. Leave at room temperature overnight.

9. Make a raspberry puree in a processor until smooth. Arrange dessert plates by putting 4 tablespoons of puree at the center of each. Place a pear on the plate and mix some syrup over it. Add a tablespoon of cream if desired.

Quickie Dulce de Leche

Indulge your sweetest craving with this very simple dessert.

Preparation Time: 25 minutes

Cooking Time: 30 minutes

Number of Servings: 6

Ingredients:

1 can of sweet condensed milk

Water

Directions:

1. Place the trivet in the pressure cooker then place the milk can in it.

2. Pour enough water until the can is covered.

3. Close the lid and bring to high pressure. Cook for 20 minutes.

4.Turn off the cooker and release the pressure naturally. Leave overnight before opening.

5.Serve with bread, or as toppings to cakes.

Cinnamon Flavored Apple Flan

Deliciously flavored flan that is so tender and tasty!

Preparation Time: 30 minutes

Cooking Time:10 minutes

Number of Servings: 6

Ingredients:

3 whole eggs

3 egg yolks

5 tablespoons maple syrup

1/4 teaspoon cinnamon

2 apples, peeled and cut in 1/4" slices

2 1/2 cups milk

6 tablespoons sugar

1/4 teaspoon vanilla

Directions:

1. In a small skillet, mix together the maple syrup and cinnamon.

2. Put in the sliced apples and cook until tender.

3. Pour the mixture in six (6) greased custard cups.

4. In a mixing bowl, beat eggs and egg yolks, and add vanilla, sugar and milk.

5.Add them to the mixture in the greased cups.

6. Wrap the 6 cups in foil. Pour in 2 ½ cups of water in the cooker and place the cups in the steamer basket.

7. Close the lid and bring to high temperature. Cook for 10 minutes.

8. Turn off the cooker and release pressure the natural way, of for 10 minutes.

9. Open the lid of the cooker, take out the cups and let them cool at room temperature.

10. Chill in the fridge before serving.

11. Enjoy!

Toffee Pudding Delight
The sweet toffee is what makes this so special.

Preparation Time: 30 minutes

Cooking Time:40 minutes

Number of Servings: 4 to 6

Ingredients:

1 large egg

2 oz. flour

2 oz. margarine

2 oz. dark muscovado sugar

2 teaspoons milk

Toffee Sauce:

1 oz. butter

2 oz. brown sugar

1 tablespoon milk

Directions:

1. In a small skillet, mix all ingredients of the toffee sauce and heat until dissolved.

2. Place 1 tablespoon of toffee sauce in a greased pudding pan.

3. In a bowl, combine egg, flour, margarine, muscovado sugar, and milk. Mix well.

3. Pour mixture into the greased pan and cover with a greaseproof paper and seal tightly.

4. In the pressure cooker, set the trivet, add 1 ¼ pints of hot water and place the greased pan with the mixture at the center of the trivet.

5. Boil uncovered for 20 minutes.

6. Close the lid and bring to high pressure. Cook for another 20 minutes.

7. Turn off the cooker and release the pressure using the slow release method.

8. Open the lid, remove the greased pan and let cool slowly.

9. Heat the leftover toffee sauce and drizzle on top of the pudding before serving.

END OF BOOK 2

BOOK 3

Electric Pressure Cooker Cookbook

Vol.3 51 Electric Pressure Cooker Soups And Stews Recipes

ROSA BARNES

142

INTRODUCTION

Soups and stews are present in almost every meal as a side dish or the main course. Whichever you may call it, young and old alike have an innate liking to this dishes that can be appropriately described as "comfort food".

I regard soup and stews as my comfort foods. When one family member is sick or ill, mother always prepares a hot bowl of soup to help ease the discomfort of our ailments. A serving of warm and savory soup is always a sure way to warm the body on wintry days and nights. A bowl of soup also waits for us as we arrive from school or work to soothe tired and aching muscles after a day's work.

I believe each of us have some "soupy" stories to tell. And these often have one thing in common, the taste of our favorite soup or stew is something unforgettable that stir up warm memories and create new ones as we finish off another bowl of soup or stew.

I remember grandma in the kitchen, patiently looking after her slow-cooking recipes, and painstakingly waiting for the beef to be tenderized, or cooked. She doesn't want her dish to be "just cooked", of course she wants it soft to perfection. It's no wonder that a lot of time is spent just cooking this favorite stew of mine.

Although pressure cookers have already been around for quite some time, my mother was wary of it due to the tales of dangers and accidents these kitchen gadgets have posed to their users. After careful consideration, she finally bought one and gave it a try. After that, kitchen life has never been the same.

Mama's wonderful pressure cooker gave us delicious food and meals that we enjoyed together as a family.

Nowadays, as busy homemakers, we are in constant search for things that will make our job easier. Just like in the kitchen, we look for gadgets or things that we know would be of great help to us, after all, they are invented for the purpose of making people's lives hassle-free and pressure-free.

That's why many enhancements to life, products and gadgets are taking place, and improvements are always welcome. The simple pressure cooker has evolved into something more useful and user friendly, while not compromising the safety of its users. More homemakers now prefer electric pressure cooker as their versatile kitchen companion.

The Pressure Cooker And The Soup

Believe it or not, you can cook almost anything in the pressure cooker! Meat, vegetables, root crops, soups and stews, desserts, jams and jellies – just name it! The secret in the successful outcome of these dishes really depends on you and how you follow the suggested cooking procedures of your cooker's manufacturer, or with the experience of other homemakers and cooks who have been using this contraption for a while now.

As versatile as a pressure cooker is, it creates a wide variety of delicious meals that makes every tummy happy. Tough cuts of meat and vegetables are cooked to perfect softness by the pressure cooker. And even better taste and aroma of food results from the air-tight cooking in this apparatus.

You have in your hands a collection of 51 carefully selected soups and stews you can cook easily in your pressure cooker. Now you can cook yummy, tasty and delightful soups and stews in a jiffy. No worries about the food being under or overcooked, the resulting dish is just about, if not always the best.

Enjoy and have fun cooking!

Rosa Barnes

SOUPS

Yummy Beef And Veggies Soup
An all-time favorite of young and old alike.

Preparation Time: 20 minutes

Cooking Time: 21 minutes

Number of Servings: 8

Ingredients:

3 lbs chuck roast

1 teaspoon butter, melted

1 tablespoon extra-virgin olive oil

7 large carrots

4 cups beef broth

6 medium potatoes, peeled and diced

8 ounces fresh mushrooms, cleaned and sliced

2 stalks celery, finely diced

1 large sweet onion, peeled and diced

10 oz frozen whole kernel corn, thawed

1 clove garlic, peeled and minced

10 oz frozen green beans, thawed

10 oz frozen baby peas, thawed

1 tablespoon dried parsley

1 bay leaf

1/4 teaspoon dried rosemary

1/4 teaspoon dried oregano

Salt and black pepper, to taste

Directions:

1. Peel the carrots. Grate 1 of the carrots and dice the remaining 6. Combine the grated carrot, mushrooms, celery, onion, butter and oil to the pressure cooker. Stir so that the vegetables are coated with butter and oil.

2. Close the lid. Bring to low pressure; cook for 1 minute. Quick-release the pressure and remove the lid.

3. Now stir in the garlic then add the broth, potatoes, diced carrots, dried parsley, bay leaf, rosemary, oregano, salt, and pepper. Trim visible fat off the roast and cut the meat into bite-sized pieces; add to the pressure cooker and stir in the vegetables. Close the lid and bring to high pressure; cook for 15 minutes. Quick-release the pressure and remove the lid.

4. Remove and discard the bay leaf. Stir in the green beans, corn, and peas; cook for 5 minutes or until the vegetables are heated through. Taste for seasoning and add additional salt, pepper, and herbs if needed.

5. Serve hot and enjoy.

Delightful Tasty Borscht
A delightful soup made all the more tasty by tomatoes.

Preparation Time: 20 minutes

Cooking Time: 21 minutes

Number of Servings: 6-8

Ingredients:

11/2 tablespoons olive oil

1 garlic clove, peeled, minced

1/2 pound lamb, cut into bite sized pieces

1 small yellow onion, peeled, diced

1 small cabbage head, chopped

1 pound of red beets

1 15-ounce can of diced tomatoes

1/4 cup of red wine vinegar

7 cups beef broth

1 tablespoon of lemon juice

2 bay leaves

4-5 beet greens

Salt and pepper to taste

Sour cream

Directions:

1. Add oil, garlic, and the lamb to pressure cooker. Brown lamb on medium heat, frequently stirring to prevent the garlic from burning. Add the onion then sauté until transparent.

2. Peel the beets and dice. Save the beet greens but rinse well and cover with cold water until required.

3. Add the cabbage, beets, tomatoes, vinegar, beef broth, lemon juice and bay leaves to the pressure cooker.

3. Close the lid and bring to low pressure; cook for 10 minutes. Remove from the heat and quick-release the pressure.

4. Chop the reserved beet greens then stir into the other ingredients in your pressure cooker.

5. Close the lid and bring to low pressure; cook for 5 minutes.

6. Remove from heat and let pressure to release naturally. Taste for seasoning then add salt and pepper to taste.

7. Transfer soup into bowls and garnish each bowl with a heaping tablespoon of sour cream.

All-Star Chicken Noodle Soup

Chicken soup never tasted this good!

Preparation Time: 20 minutes

Cooking Time: 30 minutes

Number of Servings: 6

Ingredients:

1 tablespoon oil

1 tablespoon butter

3 stalks celery, diced

6 medium carrots, peeled and sliced

1 large onion, peeled and diced

4 pounds chicken thighs and breasts

1/4 teaspoon dried thyme

1 teaspoon dried parsley

1/2 teaspoon salt

2 cups chicken broth

4 cups water

2 cups medium egg noodles

1 cup frozen baby peas, thawed

Freshly ground black pepper, to taste

Directions:

1. Melt the butter with the oil in the pressure cooker on medium heat. Add celery and carrots; sauté for 2 minutes.

2. Add onion, sauté for 3 minutes then add the chicken, thyme, parsley, salt and chicken broth.

3. Close the lid then bring to low temperature; cook for 20 minutes. Remove from the heat and quick-release the pressure. Remove the lid.

4. Transfer the chicken pieces to a cutting board using a slotted spoon to. Remove the skin and discard. Once the chicken is cool enough to handle, strip the meat from the bones then shred. Return the chicken to the pressure cooker.

5. Return the pressure cooker to medium heat. Add water, stir and bring to a boil.

6. Add the egg noodles and cook according to package directions. Stir in the thawed peas.

7. Taste and add extra salt if needed, and pepper, to taste.

Tweaked Chicken & Veggies Soup

This is a variation from the conventional chicken soup we all like.

Preparation Time: 20 minutes

Cooking Time: 21 minutes

Number of Servings: 8-10

Ingredients:

7 large carrots, 1 grated, 6 diced

2 stalks celery, finely diced

8 ounces fresh mushrooms, cleaned and sliced

1 large sweet onion, peeled and diced

1 tablespoon extra-virgin olive oil

1 teaspoon butter, melted

1 clove garlic, peeled and minced

6 medium potatoes, peeled and diced

4 cups chicken broth

1/4 teaspoon dried oregano

1 tablespoon dried parsley

1/4 teaspoon dried rosemary

1 bay leaf

2 strips orange zest

Salt and pepper to taste

8 chicken thighs, skin removed

10-ounce package frozen whole kernel corn, thawed

10-ounce package frozen green beans, thawed

10-ounce package frozen baby peas, thawed

Directions:

1. Combine the grated carrot, celery, mushrooms, onion, oil and butter in the pressure cooker. Stir to coat the vegetables with butter and oil. Close the lid. Bring to low pressure and cook for 1 minute. Quick-release the pressure and remove the lid.

2. Stir in the garlic then add the potatoes, broth, diced carrots, oregano, rosemary, dried parsley, bay leaf, orange zest, chicken thighs, salt, and pepper.

3. Close the lid then bring to high pressure. Remove from heat and let the pressure release naturally for about 5 minutes. Quick-release any remaining pressure and remove the lid.

4. Using a slotted spoon, remove the chicken thighs then strip the meat from the bone. Cut into bite-sizes then return to the pot. Remove and discard the orange zest and bay leaf. Return the uncovered pressure cooker to medium heat.

5. Stir in the corn, green beans and peas; cook for 5 minutes or until the vegetables are heated through. Taste for seasoning and add additional salt, pepper, and herbs if needed.

Sweet And Creamy Corn Chowder

Creamy and nutritious corn chowder.

Preparation Time: 20 minutes

Cooking Time: 21 minutes

Number of Servings: 6

Ingredients:

2 tablespoons butter

4 large leeks

2 cups water

4 cups vegetable stock

6 medium potatoes, peeled and diced

Salt and pepper to taste

1 bay leaf

1 1/2 cups fresh or frozen corn

Pinch sugar

1/2 teaspoon dried thyme

1/2 cup heavy cream, or unsweetened soymilk

Directions:

1. Add butter to the pressure cooker and melt over medium heat. Cut off the root end of each leek then discard outer leaves that are bruised. Slice the leeks then sauté in the pressure cooker for 2 minutes

2. Stir in the water, stock, potatoes, salt, pepper and the bay leaf.

3. Close the lid, bring to high pressure and cook for 4 minutes. Quick-release the pressure and remove the lid. Remove the bay leaf and discard it.

4. Stir in the corn, sugar, thyme and cream. Bring to temperature with occasional stirring.

DIY Manhattan Style Clam Chowder

The clams and their liquid will be salty, so wait until the chowder is cooked to add any salt. Serve with oyster crackers, dinner rolls, or toasted garlic bread.

Preparation Time: 20 minutes

Cooking Time: 21 minutes

Number of Servings: 6

Ingredients:

4 6-1/2 ounce cans, minced clams

4 slices bacon

4 large carrots, peeled and finely diced

2 stalks celery, finely diced

1 large sweet onion, peeled and diced

1 pound red potatoes, peeled and diced

2 cups tomato or V-8 juice

1 28-ounce can diced tomatoes

1/4 teaspoon dried thyme

1 teaspoon dried parsley

1/8 teaspoon dried oregano

1/2 teaspoon freshly ground black pepper

Sea salt, to taste

Directions:

1. Drain the clams and reserve the liquid. Set clams aside.

2. Dice the bacon, add it the pressure cooker and fry over medium-high heat until crisp enough to crumble.

3. Add the carrots and celery; sauté for about 3 minutes. Add the onion and sauté for 3 minutes or until translucent.

4. Add the potatoes; stir-fry briefly in the bacon fat and vegetable mixture so that potatoes are coated in the fat.

5. Stir in the tomato or V-8 juice, undrained tomatoes, clam liquid, thyme, parsley, oregano, and pepper.

6. Close the lid, bring to high pressure and cook for 5 minutes. Lower the heat to warm then allow pressure to go down naturally for 10 minutes. Quick-release remaining pressure and then remove the lid.

7. Stir in the reserved clams then bring to a simmer. Simmer for 5 minutes or until the clams are heated through (but do not boil). Taste for seasoning and add salt if you like.

Creamy Clam Chowder New England Style

This is really nice if you are a fan of clams.

Preparation Time: 30 minutes

Cooking Time: 30 minutes

Number of Servings: 4

Ingredients:

4 61/2-ounce cans chopped clams

4 slices bacon

2 large shallots, peeled and minced

1 stalk celery, finely diced

1 pound red potatoes, peeled and diced

1 tablespoon fresh thyme, chopped

2 1/2 cups unsalted chicken or vegetable broth

1 cup frozen corn, thawed

1 cup heavy cream

2 cups milk

Sea Salt and pepper to taste

Directions:

1. Drain the clams and reserve the liquid. Set clams aside.

2. Dice the bacon, add it the pressure cooker and fry over medium-high heat until crisp enough to crumble.

3. Add the shallots and celery; sauté for about 3 minutes. Add the potatoes; stir-fry briefly in the bacon fat and vegetable mixture so that potatoes are coated in the fat. Stir in thyme, broth and clam liquid.

4. Close the lid, bring to high pressure and cook for 5 minutes. Lower the heat to warm then allow pressure to go down naturally for 10 minutes. Quick-release remaining pressure and then remove the lid.

5. Stir in the reserved clams, corn, cream and milk then bring to a simmer. Let simmer for 5 minutes or until the clams are heated through (but do not boil). Taste for seasoning and add salt if you like.

Winter Night Salmon Chowder
Fish in a chowder provides insulation and warm comfort on cold nights.

Preparation Time: 10 minutes

Cooking Time: 15 minutes

Number of Servings: 4

Ingredients:

4 6-ounce salmon fillets, skin removed

4 teaspoons freshly squeezed lemon juice

1 tablespoon olive or vegetable oil

1 large leek

4 medium Yukon Gold potatoes, peeled and diced

1 large fennel bulb

4 cups water

1 teaspoon sea salt

1 bay leaf

Directions:

1. Drizzle 1/2 teaspoon of lemon juice on each side of each salmon fillet. Set fillets aside.

2. Heat oil in the pressure cooker on medium heat.

3. Trim, slice thinly, wash and then drain the leek. Pat dry with paper towels if necessary.

4. Add the leek to the pressure cooker and sauté for about 2 minutes.

5. Slice fennel bulb into quarters, then slice the quarters thinly. Combine the fennel, diced potatoes, water, salt and bay leaf in the pressure cooker.

6. Close the lid and bring to high pressure; cook for 7 minutes. Quick-release the pressure and remove the lid.

7. Add the salmon fillets to the pressure cooker. Close the lid again, bring to high pressure and cook for 1 minute. Remove from heat then allow pressure to release naturally.

8. Remove the bay leaf and discard. Lift each salmon fillet into a bowl using a slotted spoon.

9. Taste the chowder for seasoning and add salt as needed. Spoon the chowder into bowls.

Pressure Cooker Seafood Chowder

Seafood comes to life in this simple but elegant meal.

Preparation Time: 20 minutes

Cooking Time: 21 minutes

Number of Servings: 6

Ingredients:

2 tablespoons butter

2 large leeks

2 cups water

4 cups clam juice or fish broth

6 medium russet, peeled and diced

1 bay leaf

Salt and pepper to taste

1 pound scrod or other firm whitefish

1/2 cup heavy cream

1/2 teaspoon dried thyme

Directions:

1. Melt butter in your pressure cooker on medium heat. Cut off root ends of the leek, discard bruised outer leaves then slice the leeks.

2. Rinse under running water to get rid of dirt; drain and dry. Add to pressure cooker then sauté in the butter for about 2 minutes. Stir in the water, broth and potatoes. Add the bay leaf then season with salt and pepper.

3. Close the lid, bring to high pressure and cook for 4 minutes. Quick-release the pressure and then remove the lid. Discard the bay leaf.

4. Cut the fish into bite-sized pieces and add to the pressure cooker. Let simmer for about 3 minutes or until the fish becomes opaque and flakes easily. Stir in the cream and thyme.

5. Leave the pan on the heat, occasionally stirring, until the cream comes to temperature. Taste for seasoning; add additional salt and pepper if needed.

Easy Chestnut Cream Soup

A small serving of this creamy soup is a delightful way to start any meal.

Preparation Time: 15 minutes

Cooking Time: 50 minutes

Number of Servings: 8

Ingredients:

1/2 pound dried chestnuts

3 tablespoons butter

1 sprig sage

1 onion, roughly sliced

1 stalk celery, roughly chopped

1/4 teaspoon white pepper

4 cups chicken broth

1 medium potato, peeled and roughly chopped

159

1 bay leaf

1/4 teaspoon ground nutmeg

2 tablespoons dark rum

Directions:

1. Cover dry chestnuts with water in a large bowl. Place in the refrigerator to soak overnight then drain and rinse. If you want to use canned chestnuts, drain and rinse also.

2. Add butter to uncovered pressure cooker and melt on medium heat.

Add the sage, onion, celery and pepper then sauté until onions are soft. Add broth, chestnuts, potato and bay leaf. Lock the lid in place.

3.Turn up to high heat and when the cooker gets to pressure, lower to minimum heat required to cook. Cook for 15 to 20 minutes at high pressure.

4. Open with the natural-release method. Disengage the "keep warm" mode or unplug the cooker. After 10 minutes, release the rest of the pressure using the valve.

5. Remove and discard the bay leaf then add nutmeg and rum. Use an immersion blender to purée the contents of the pressure cooker.

Healthy Mushroom Cream Soup
Another all-time favorite. Creamy and delicious!

Preparation Time: 20 minutes

Cooking Time: 21 minutes

Number of Servings: 4

Ingredients:

1/4 cup butter

1 yellow onion, diced

2 potatoes, peeled and diced

2 cups white mushrooms, sliced

2 cloves garlic, minced

3 cups milk

1/4 cup white wine

1 cup béchamel sauce

1 teaspoon dried thyme

Salt and pepper, to taste

Directions:

1. In the pressure cooker, sauté onions in butter until golden brown. Add the potatoes, mushrooms, and garlic and sauté for another 5 minutes.

2. Add the soymilk, white wine, béchamel sauce and thyme.

3. Close the lid and bring to high pressure. Once it gets to pressure, turn to low heat and cook for 8 minutes. Remove from the heat and let pressure release naturally.

4. Purée the soup in a blender or food processor. Taste for seasoning then add salt and pepper as needed.

Grandma's Asparagus Cream Soup
This is the best soup in the land according to my grandma.

Preparation Time: 10 minutes

Cooking Time: 12 minutes

Number of Servings: 4-6

Ingredients:

2 tablespoons butter

2 pounds asparagus

1 large onion, diced

1 1/2 teaspoons salt

1/8 teaspoon cayenne pepper

5 cups vegetable stock

1 teaspoon lemon juice

1/4 cup milk

Directions:

1. Trim off the hard ends of the asparagus and cut it into 1 inch pieces. Sauté onion in the pressure cooker until golden brown. Add the asparagus, cayenne pepper and salt then sauté for 5 minutes.

2. Next the vegetable stock. Close the lid and bring to high pressure. Once it gets to pressure, turn to low heat and cook for 5 minutes.

3. Remove from the heat and let the pressure release naturally. Add the lemon juice and milk to the soup then purée in a blender or food processor.

Creamiest Lima Bean Soup

Mouthwatering soup, made with lima beans. Yummy!

Preparation Time: 20 minutes   plus 8 hours cooking time

Cooking Time: 9-10 minutes

Number of Servings: 4-6

Ingredients:

2 cups dried lima beans

Water for soaking lima beans, plus 1/2 cup

2 cups vegetable stock

1 tablespoon olive oil

1 clove garlic, minced

1 small onion, diced

Salt and pepper, to taste

2 tablespoons chives, sliced

Directions:

1. Rinse lima beans, cover in water in a bowl and let soak for 8 hours. Drain.

2. Sauté the onion in hot oil in the pressure cooker. Add garlic and cook for an extra minute.

3. Add lima beans, 1/2 cup water and vegetable stock. Close the lid and bring to high pressure. Cook for 6 minutes. Remove from the heat and let the pressure release naturally.

4. Purée the soup in a blender or food processor.

5. Season with salt and pepper, and garnish with chives before serving.

Garlicky Northern Bean Soup
Garlic adds a special touch to this soup.

Preparation Time: 20 minutes plus 8 hours soaking time

Cooking Time: 15 minutes

Number of Servings: 8

Ingredients:

2 cups dried great northern beans

Water, as needed

3 tablespoons olive oil

6 cloves garlic, minced

1 onion, sliced

6 cups vegetable stock

1 tablespoon rosemary, chopped

1 bay leaf

1 teaspoon lemon juice

Salt and pepper, to taste

Directions:

1. Rinse beans, cover in water in a bowl and let soak for 8 hours. Drain.

2. Heat oil in your pressure cooker on medium heat. Sauté onion until golden brown, add garlic and sauté for another 1 minute.

3. Add the vegetable stock, rosemary and the bay leaf.

4. Close the lid and bring to high pressure. Cook for about10 minutes. Remove from the heat and let the pressure release naturally.

5. Remove the bay leaf and discard. Purée the soup in a blender or food processor. Add the lemon juice. Add salt and pepper if needed.

Pressure Cooked Black Bean Soup
Savor the delicious taste of this bean soup with the smoky flavor of sausage.

Preparation Time: 15 minutes

Cooking Time: 1 hour

Number of Servings: 8

Ingredients:

1/2 pound bacon, chopped

1 green bell pepper, seeded, diced

2 medium yellow onion, peeled, diced

8 ounces of smoked sausage, diced

3 garlic cloves, peeled, minced

1/2 teaspoon ground cumin

2 teaspoons paprika

1/4 teaspoon coriander

1/2 teaspoon chili powder

1 bay leaf

6 cups of chicken broth or water

1 smoked turkey wing or smoked ham hock

1 pound dried black beans, soaked overnight, rinsed, drained

1/8 teaspoon dried red pepper flakes

1/2 cup dry sherry

1 tablespoon red wine vinegar

Salt and pepper to taste

Directions:

1. Add bacon to your pressure cooker then fry on medium-high heat until bacon starts to release its fat. Reduce to medium heat, and green pepper and sauté for 3 minutes.

2. Stir in the onion and smoked sausage. Sauté for 3 minutes or until onion is soft. Next stir in the garlic, cumin, paprika, coriander, chili powder, bay leaf, water or broth, turkey wing or ham hock and beans.

3. Close the lid, bring to high pressure and cook for 30 minutes. Remove from heat and allow the pressure to naturally release, leaving the lid on for at least 20 minutes. Remove the lid.

4. Take out the turkey wing or ham hock and strip the meat off of the bones. Return the meat to the pot. Remove the bay leaf and discard. Puree the soup partially with an immersion blender or potato masher.

5. Return the uncovered pot to medium heat then bring to a simmer. Stir in the dried red pepper flakes or cayenne pepper , vinegar and sherry. Simmer for 20 minutes.

6. Taste for seasoning then add salt and pepper if needed. You may also add more herbs, chili powder, and red pepper flakes or cayenne pepper if you like.

Chickpea And Curry Broth

Making this soup as spicy as you want is a matter of choice. But one thing is sure, it's tasty!

Preparation Time: 15 minutes   plus 8 minutes soaking time

Cooking Time: 30 minutes

Number of Servings: 8

Ingredients:

2 cups dried chickpeas

Water

3 tablespoons olive oil

1/2 onion, diced

1 teaspoon garam masala

1 teaspoon fresh ginger

2 garlic cloves, minced

2-3 teaspoons curry powder

1 14-ounce can coconut milk

2 cups vegetable stock

Salt and pepper, to taste

Directions:

1. Rinse chickpeas, cover in water in a bowl and let soak for 8 hours. Drain.

2. Add olive oil to the pressure cooker then sauté onion until golden brown.

3. Add the garam masala, ginger, garlic and curry powder then sauté for 1 minute more.

4. Add the coconut milk and stock. Close the lid and bring to high pressure. Maintain for 20 minutes then remove from the heat. Let the pressure release naturally.

5. Purée the soup in a blender or food processor. Taste for seasoning then add salt and pepper, if required.

Chinese Egg Drop Soup
This is very simple but not in the taste, it is simply excellent.

Preparation Time: 5 minutes

Cooking Time: 15 minutes

Number of Servings: 6

Ingredients:

1 star anise

1/2 teaspoon ginger

3 fennel seeds

2 cloves

2 teaspoons white pepper

1/8 teaspoon cinnamon

167

2 cups chicken broth

4 cups water

8 ounces cherry tomatoes, halved

4 eggs, whisked

2 green scallions, chopped

Directions:

1. Combine the spices (star anise, ginger, fennel seeds, cloves, white pepper and cinnamon) in a bouquet garni bag or tea ball. Add the bag of spices, broth, water and tomatoes to the pressure cooker. Close the lid and lock.

2.Turn the heat up to high. When the cooker gets to pressure, lower the minimum heat required for maintaining pressure. Cook for 5–7 minutes at high pressure.

3. Release pressure and open the pressure cooker.

4. Stir clockwise with one hand and slowly pour in the whisked eggs with your other, creating thin strands.

5. Sprinkle with the green scallions and serve.

Onion Soup French Style
Onion and red wine combined brings out the best in this broth.

Preparation Time: 15 minutes

Cooking Time: 20 minutes

Number of Servings: 4

Ingredients:

1/4 cup olive oil

4 Vidalia onions, sliced

4 cloves garlic, minced

4 cups vegetable stock

1 cup red wine

1 tablespoon dried thyme

Salt and pepper, to taste

4 slices French bread

4 ounces Swiss cheese

Directions:

1. Add olive oil to the pressure cooker on medium-high heat and sauté the onions until light brown. Stir in the garlic and sauté for 1 minute.

2. Add the vegetable stock, red wine and thyme.

3. Close the lid and bring to high pressure. Once it gets to pressure, turn the heat to low then cook for about 10 minutes. Remove from the heat and let the pressure release naturally for 20 minutes. Quick-release remaining pressure and then remove the lid.

4. Taste for seasoning then add salt and pepper if needed.

5. Toast the slices of French bread lightly in the oven broiler. To serve, ladle the soup into broiler-safe bowls, place one slice of toasted French bread on top of the soup then place a slice of the cheese on top of the bread. Place the soup bowl under the broiler until the cheese has melted.

Sweet And Sour Tomato Soup

Celebrate summer with this sweet and sour concoction.

Preparation Time: 10 minutes

Cooking Time: 10 minutes

Number of Servings: 4

Ingredients:

169

8 medium fresh tomatoes

1 cup water

1/4 teaspoon sea salt

1/2 teaspoon baking soda

2 cups heavy cream or milk

Freshly ground black pepper, to taste

Directions:

1. Wash the tomatoes then peel, seed and dice. Add tomato along with juice to the pressure cooker. Add water and salt then stir and close the lid.

2. Bring the pressure cooker to low pressure over medium heat; cook for 2 minutes. Quick-release the pressure and remove the lid.

3. Stir the baking soda into the tomato mixture. Once it's stopped foaming and bubbling, stir in cream or milk.

4. Cook with stirring for several minutes or until the soup is heated through. Add pepper, to taste.

Meatball Soup Greek Version
This dish is an adaptation of a Greek soup I once tasted on holiday.

Preparation Time: 15 minutes

Cooking Time: 20 minutes

Number of Servings: 6

Ingredients:

1/4 pound ground pork

1 pound lean ground beef

6 tablespoons uncooked converted long-grain white rice

1 small onion, peeled and minced

1 clove garlic, peeled and minced

1 tablespoon dried parsley

2 teaspoons dried mint

1 teaspoon dried oregano

Salt and pepper to taste

3 large eggs

6 cups chicken broth or water

1 cup baby carrots, each sliced into thirds

1 medium onion, peeled and chopped

1 stalk celery, finely chopped

2 large potatoes, peeled and cut into cubes

2 tablespoons corn flour

1/3 cup fresh lemon juice

Directions:

1. In a large bowl, combine the meat, rice, onion, garlic, parsley, mint, oregano, salt, pepper, and 1 of the eggs. Using your hands, shape into small meatballs and then set aside.

2. Add 2 cups of either water or broth to the pressure cooker. Add the meatballs, carrots, onion, celery and potatoes, and then pour in the remaining water or broth to cover the vegetables and meatballs.

3. Close the lid, bring to low pressure and cook for 10 minutes. Remove from the heat and allow the pressure to release naturally. Remove the lid.

4. Using a slotted spoon, move the meatballs to a soup tureen; cover and keep warm.

5. Return the pot to medium heat and bring to a simmer. In a measuring cup or small bowl, beat the two remaining eggs, then whisk in the corn flour. Gradually whisk in lemon juice.

6. Scoop in about 1 cup of hot broth from the pressure cooker. Do this in a slow and steady stream while continuously beating until the hot liquid is fully integrated into the egg-corn flour mixture. Now stir this mixture into the pressure cooker.

7. Stir and simmer for about 5 minutes or until the mixture is thickened. Taste for seasoning and adjust if necessary.

8. Pour over the meatballs and serve.

Pasta And Italian Bean Soup

Pasta and bean together in this Italian soup? Let's give it a try.

Preparation Time: 20 minutes   plus 8 hours soaking time

Cooking Time: 12 minutes

Number of Servings: 10

Ingredients:

1 pound dried cannellini beans

6 cups water plus more, as required

1 tablespoon olive oil

2 stalks celery, diced

4 medium carrots, peeled and diced

2 medium onions, peeled and diced

1 teaspoon dried oregano

3 cloves garlic, peeled and minced

172

1 teaspoon dried basil

1 bay leaf

1 teaspoon dried parsley

4 cups mushroom broth or vegetable stock

11/2 cups small shell pasta or small macaroni

Salt and pepper to taste

Directions:

1. Rinse cannellini, cover in water in a bowl and let soak for 8 hours. Drain.

2. Heat oil in the pressure cooker on medium heat. Add the celery and carrots ; sauté for 3 minutes. Add onion and sauté for 3 minutes or until soft. Add the oregano, garlic and basil then sauté for 30 seconds.

3. Add 6 cups of water, beans, and bay leaf. Close the lid and bring to high pressure; cook for 10 minutes. Remove from the heat and let the pressure release naturally.

4. Remove and discard the bay leaf. Add the parsley, and mushroom broth or vegetable stock. Return to the heat and bring to a boil; stir in the macaroni or shells.

5. Cook pasta to al dente following package directions. Taste for seasoning and add salt and pepper if necessary.

Easy Lentil Soup
Lentils of any color can be used for this soup.

Preparation Time: 20 minutes

Cooking Time: 21 minutes

Number of Servings: 4-6

Ingredients:

1 tablespoon olive oil

1 yellow onion, sliced

1 carrot, sliced

4 cloves garlic, minced

5 plum tomatoes, chopped

2 teaspoons dried tarragon

1 teaspoon dried thyme

1 teaspoon paprika

6 cups vegetable stock

2 cups lentils

2 bay leaves

Salt and pepper, to taste

Directions:

1. Add oil to the pressure cooker on medium heat. Sauté onion in hot oil until golden. Add carrot and garlic and sauté for 2–3 minutes more.

2. Add the remaining ingredients except for salt and pepper. Close the lid and bring to high pressure. Once it gets to pressure, turn to low heat and cook for 8 minutes.

3. Remove from the heat and allow the pressure to release naturally.

4. Remove the bay leaves and add salt and pepper to taste.

Mushroom And Barley Soup

Mushrooms and barley in this dish, make a tasteful combination!

Preparation Time: 20 minutes

Cooking Time: 21 minutes

Number of Servings: 6

Ingredients:

1 tablespoon olive or vegetable oil

2 tablespoons butter

1 large carrot, peeled and diced

2 stalks celery, diced

1 large sweet onion, peeled, halved, and sliced

8 ounces button mushrooms, cleaned and sliced

1 portobello mushroom cap, diced

2 cloves garlic, peeled and minced

1/2 cup pearled barley

1 bay leaf

6 cups water

Salt and pepper to taste

Directions:

1. Add butter and oil to pressure cooker on medium heat. When the butter has melted, add carrot and celery and sauté for about 2 minutes. Add the onion then sauté for 3 minutes or until soft and translucent.

2. Stir in the mushrooms and garlic; sauté for 5 minutes or until the onion begins to turn golden and mushrooms release their moisture.

3. Stir in the barley, bay leaf and water. Close the lid and bring to high pressure; cook for 20 minutes. Remove from the heat then allow pressure to release naturally.

4. Remove the lid. Remove the bay leaf and discard. Taste for seasoning and add salt and pepper if needed.

Classic Potato Soup
What can lighten up a chilly morning? This potato soup surely will.

Preparation Time: 10 minutes

Cooking Time: 40 minutes

Number of Servings: 4

Ingredients:

1/4 cup olive oil

1/2 cup celery, sliced

1/2 cup onion, diced

3 cups vegetable stock

4 cups potatoes, peeled and diced

2 cups béchamel sauce

Salt and pepper, to taste

Directions:

1. Heat oil on medium heat in the pressure cooker and sauté the celery and onion for about 5 minutes. Add the vegetable stock and potatoes.

2. Close the lid and bring to high pressure. Once it gets to pressure, turn to low heat and cook for 8-10 minutes. Remove from the heat and let the pressure release naturally for about 20 minutes. Quick-release any remaining pressure then remove the lid.

3. Bring the soup to a simmer in the pressure cooker and gradually stir in the béchamel sauce to thicken.

4.Taste for seasoning then add salt and pepper if required. Garnish with parsley or chives.

Chickpea And Pasta Soup
Thick and healthy soup, delicious and tasty, what more can one ask for?

Preparation Time: 20 minutes

Cooking Time: 21 minutes

Number of Servings: 6

Ingredients:

1 cup dried chickpeas

7 cups water, divided

1 tablespoon olive oil

1 carrot, chopped

1 celery stalk, chopped

1 onion, chopped

1 sprig sage

1 sprig rosemary

1 clove garlic, pressed

1 bay leaf

1 spoon of tomato concentrate or 2 tablespoons tomato purée

3 cups water

1 cup pasta, small shape

1 teaspoon pepper

Directions:

1. Soak chickpeas in 4 cups of water for at least 24 hours. Drain then set aside.

2. Heat olive oil in an uncovered pressure cooker on medium heat. Sauté the carrot, celery and onion until softened. Add sage, rosemary, garlic and bay leaf then stir for about a minute. Then add the 3 cups water, tomato purée and garbanzo beans.. Close and lock the lid.

3. Turn up to high heat and when the cooker reaches pressure, lower to the minimum heat needed to cook. Cook for 13–18 minutes at high pressure.

4. Open with the natural-release method—disengage the "keep warm" mode or unplug the cooker and open when the pressure indicator has gone down (20–30 minutes).

5. Bring the contents of the pressure cooker to a boil, uncovered, and add the pasta. Cook for about 8–10 minutes or until the pasta is tender,.

6. Season with salt and pepper before serving.

Hearty Kale Soup
Kale can easily become your favorite from now on after having a serving of this.

Preparation Time: 20 minutes   plus 1 hour soaking time

Cooking Time: 15 minutes

Number of Servings: 6

Ingredients:

1 pound kale

1 tablespoon of olive oil

1 medium yellow onion, peeled, sliced thinly

1/2 pound kielbasa or linguica, sliced

4 cups of chicken broth

4 large potatoes, peeled, diced

2 15-ounce cans of cannellini beans, rinsed and drained

Salt and pepper to taste

Directions:

1. Trim off the large ribs of the kale then slice it into thin strips. Transfer kale strips into a bowl of cold water allow to soak for an hour; drain well.

2. Stir together the oil, onions, and kielbasa or linguica in the pressure cooker. Set on medium heat and sauté for 5 minutes until onions are soft. Add the chicken broth, potatoes, beans and drained kale.

3. Close the lid, bring to low pressure and cook for 8 minutes. Remove from the heat and let the pressure release naturally for 5 minutes. Quick-release remaining pressure and remove the lid.

4.Taste for seasoning then add salt and pepper to taste.

Traditional Mexican Posole

Preparation Time: 20 minutes   plus 1 hour soaking time

Cooking Time: 28 minutes

Number of Servings: 8

Ingredients:

8 cups water

2 cups hominy

2 tablespoons olive oil

2 zucchini, diced

2 yellow squash, diced

1/2 onion, diced

2 cloves garlic, minced

1 cup tomato, diced

2 dried Ancho chilies

2 bay leaves

8 cups vegetable stock

2 teaspoons dried oregano

1 teaspoon dried thyme

1 teaspoon saffron

1 teaspoon salt

1 tablespoon lime juice

1 avocado, pitted and sliced

Directions:

1. In the pressure cooker, combine the hominy with 4 cups of water. Close the lid; bring to high pressure for a minute. Remove from the heat then quick-release the pressure.

2. Drain the water then rinse the hominy with fresh water and return to pressure cooker with the remaining 4 cups of water. Allow to soak for 1 hour then drain and set aside.

3. Heat olive oil on medium heat in the pressure cooker. Add zucchini, squash and onion; sauté for about 5 minutes. Add garlic and sauté for 30 seconds more.

4. Next stir in all remaining ingredients except for avocado. Close the lid; bring to high pressure and maintain for 20 minutes. Remove from heat and let pressure release naturally.

5. Spoon into bowls and top each with 1/8 of the sliced avocado.

Hearty Split Pea Soup

This hearty soup can be served as a meal by itself. Yummy!

Preparation Time: 10 minutes

Cooking Time: 30 minutes

Number of Servings: 6

Ingredients:

4 strips bacon, diced

1 large sweet onion, peeled and diced

2 large potatoes, peeled and diced

1 cup dried green split peas, rinsed

2 large carrots, peeled and sliced

2 smoked ham hocks

4 cups chicken broth

Salt and pepper to taste

Directions:

1. Add the bacon to the pressure cooker and fry over medium heat until it begins to render its fat.

2. Add the onion then sauté for 3 minutes or until soft. Add diced potatoes; sauté for 3 minutes. Add the split peas, carrots, ham hocks and broth.

3.Close the lid, bring to low pressure; cook for 15 minutes. Remove from the heat and let the pressure release naturally.

4. Remove the lid. Remove the ham hocks using a slotted spoon then allow to cool until the meat can be removed from the bones. Taste the split peas and if they are not cooked through, close the lid and cook at low pressure for 5 minutes more. Remove from the heat and quick-release the pressure.

5. When the split peas are cooked through and tender, stir the ham you removed from the hocks into the soup. Pureé the soup with an immersion blender if desired.

6. Return the soup to medium heat and bring to a simmer. Taste for seasoning and add salt and pepper if needed.

Thai Style Coconut-Carrot Soup
This is a very rich soup, and a delicious one at that.

Preparation Time: 10 minutes

Cooking Time: 8 minutes

Number of Servings: 8-10

Ingredients:

1 tablespoon olive oil

1 onion, diced

3 teaspoons curry powder

2 cloves garlic, minced

1 pound carrots, peeled and roughly chopped

1 bay leaf

4 cups vegetable stock

1 cup unsweetened coconut milk

1 teaspoon salt

1/2 teaspoon pepper

1/4 cup basil, thinly sliced

Directions:

1. In an uncovered pressure cooker, heat olive oil on medium heat. Sauté the onion until soft. Add curry powder and the garlic and sauté for 30 seconds more. Next add the rest of the ingredients except basil. Close and lock the lid.

2. Turn up to high heat and when the cooker gets to pressure, lower the heat to the minimum needed for cooking. Cook for 5–7 minutes at high pressure.

3. Open with the natural-release method -disengage the "keep warm" mode or unplug the cooker. After 10 minutes, release the rest of the pressure using the valve.

4. Remove the bay leaf then pureé the soup using an immersion blender. Add salt and pepper. Garnish individual bowls with basil.

Pressure Cooker Tortilla Soup

Enjoy this soup with… what else but tortillas?

Preparation Time: 15 minutes

Cooking Time: 27 minutes

Number of Servings: 6-8

Ingredients:

2 tablespoons olive oil

2 cloves garlic, minced

1 large onion, chopped

7 cups vegetable stock

2 tablespoons soy sauce

1 cup corn kernels

2 cups tomato, diced

1 teaspoon cayenne pepper

1 teaspoon chipotle powder

2 teaspoons ground cumin

1 teaspoon dried oregano

2 teaspoons salt

10 small corn tortillas, sliced

8 ounces shredded cheese

Directions:

1. Add the olive oil to the pressure cooker then sauté onion and garlic until light brown.

2. Add the stock, soy sauce, corn, tomato, cayenne, chipotle powder, cumin, oregano and salt. Stir to combine.

3. Close the lid; bring to medium pressure and maintain pressure for 15 minutes. Remove from the heat and quick-release the pressure.

4. Meanwhile, slice the corn tortillas into thin strips and place on an ungreased baking sheet. Bake in the oven at 450°F for about 10 minutes, or until they become golden brown. Remove from heat then set aside.

5. Purée the soup using a regular or immersion blender.

6. Serve with cooked tortilla strips and 1 ounce of shredded cheese on each soup bowl.

STEWS

Curried Peanut Stew

Inspired by the African style of peanut stew, try this for a tasty treat.

Preparation Time: 20 minutes

Cooking Time: 21 minutes

Number of Servings: 8

Ingredients:

1 tablespoon peanut oil

1 red bell pepper, diced

1 cup onion, diced

2 tablespoons fresh ginger, minced

2 cloves garlic, minced

1 14-ounce can diced tomatoes, drained

1 sweet potato, peeled, cubed

1 14-ounce can chickpeas, drained

1/2 cup chunky peanut butter

3 cups vegetable stock

1 tablespoon curry powder

1 teaspoon salt

1/2 teaspoon of black pepper

1/2 cup coconut milk

Directions:

1. Heat oil in the pressure cooker on medium heat. Sauté red bell pepper and onion for 3 minutes. Add the ginger and garlic, then sauté for 30 seconds more.

2. Combine the tomatoes, sweet potato, chickpeas, peanut butter, stock, curry powder, salt, and pepper in the pressure cooker. Close and lock the lid; bring to high pressure then maintain for 10 minutes. Remove from the heat and let the pressure release naturally.

3. Stir in the coconut milk prior to serving.

Stewed Lamb

Lamb stew is always special and can be prepared anytime of the day.

Preparation Time: 15 minutes

Cooking Time: 32 minutes

Number of Servings: 6

Ingredients:

1 tablespoon olive oil

2 pounds boneless lamb shoulder, cut to bite-sized pieces

2 cloves garlic, peeled, minced

1 large onion, peeled, diced

1/2 cup blanched whole almonds

1 cup dried apricots, cut in halve

1/3 cup raisins

1 tablespoon fresh ginger, minced

1/2 teaspoon ground cinnamon

3/4 cup red wine

1/4 cup freshly squeezed orange juice

1/2 cup fresh mint leaves, packed

Salt and freshly ground black pepper, to taste

Directions:

1. Heat the oil over medium-high heat in the pressure cooker.

2. Working in batches, brown lamb in hot oil for about 5 minutes or until properly browned. Remove with a slotted spoon and set aside, covered with foil.

3. Sauté onion for 3 minutes in the pressure cooker. Next stir in the garlic and sauté for 30 seconds.

4. Add almonds, apricots, raisins, ginger, cinnamon, wine, orange juice, and mint to the pressure cooker.

5. Lock the lid, bring to high pressure then maintain pressure for about 20 min. Remove from the heat and let the pressure release naturally.

6. Now remove the lid, stir, and taste for seasoning. Add salt and pepper to taste. Garnish with fresh mint leaves if desired.

Stewed Potato And Kale
Bring home the goodness of potatoes in this tasty stew.

Preparation Time: 15 minutes

Cooking Time: 16 minutes

Number of Servings: 4

Ingredients:

3 cups kale, chopped

1 tablespoon olive oil

2 cloves garlic, minced

3 cups vegetable stock

4 red potatoes, peeled, quartered

1 teaspoon salt

1 teaspoon black pepper

1 14-ounce can whole tomatoes, drained

2 15-ounce cans cannellini beans, drained

Directions:

1. Trim the tough stalk end off each kale leaf, then chop the leaves into large pieces.

2. Heat olive oil on medium heat in your pressure cooker then sauté garlic for 30 seconds.

3. Add all remaining ingredients. Close and lock the lid, bring to high pressure and maintain for 15 minutes. Remove from heat and let the pressure release naturally.

Beef And Beer Stew
This flavorful stew is filled with the goodness of vegetables.

Preparation Time: 15 minutes

Cooking Time: 32 minutes

Number of Servings: 8

Ingredients:

2 teaspoons canola oil

2 carrots, diced

1 large onion, diced

3 cloves garlic, minced

2 parsnips, diced

2 tablespoons minced fresh rosemary

2 stalks celery, diced

2 russet potatoes, peeled and diced

2 pounds lean top round roast, cut into 1 cubes

1 teaspoon salt

1/2 teaspoon pepper

1 teaspoon unsweetened cocoa powder

1 tablespoon honey

11/2 cups Guinness extra stout beer

1 cup frozen peas

Directions:

1. Heat oil in an uncovered pressure cooker on medium heat. Add carrots, onion, garlic, parsnips, rosemary, celery, potatoes and beef. Sauté until softened and brown. Drain the excess fat. Add salt, pepper, cocoa powder and honey. Pour in the beer. Close the lid and lock.

2. Turn up to high heat and when the cooker reaches pressure, lower the heat to the minimum required to maintain pressure. Cook for 13–15 minutes at high pressure.

3. Open the pressure cooker by releasing pressure.

4. Add the peas then let simmer uncovered for 5 minutes before you serve.

Sweet Corn & Sausage Stew

The taste of corn and sausage makes this stew the magical solution to cold summer nights.

Preparation Time: 10 minutes

Cooking Time: 10 minutes

Number of Servings: 6

Ingredients:

1 pound red potatoes, whole and unpeeled

1/4 cup Old Bay seasoning

12 cups water

1 14-ounce package Tofurky sausage cut into 2 pieces

6 ears corn on the cob, husked, cleaned, halved

2 whole heads garlic

Directions:

1. In the pressure cooker, combine potatoes, Old Bay and water. Close and lock the lid, bring to high pressure then maintain for 5 minutes. Quick-release the pressure.

2. Next, add all remaining ingredients, Close and lock the lid again, bring to high pressure and maintain for 5 another minutes. Remove from heat and let the pressure release naturally.

3. Drain the liquid before serving or remove the Tofurky sausage and vegetables with a slotted spoon.

Dark Beer Chicken Stew

Preparation Time: 15 minutes

Cooking Time: 50 minutes

Number of Servings: 6

Ingredients:

2 tablespoons unbleached all-purpose flour

1 teaspoon salt

1/2 teaspoon cayenne pepper

1/2 tablespoon garlic powder

2 pounds chicken thighs, boneless, skinless

2 tablespoons olive

1 stalk celery, diced

1 small red bell pepper, seeded and diced

1 small green bell pepper, seeded and diced

1 medium onion, peeled and diced

2 cloves garlic, peeled and minced

1 jalapeño pepper, seeded and diced

1 12-ounce bottle dark beer

2 teaspoons Worcestershire sauce

1 8-ounce can tomato sauce

1/2 cup chicken broth

1 teaspoon marjoram

1 bay leaf

1 tablespoon lard or bacon fat

Freshly ground black pepper, to taste

Directions:

1. In a large resealable bag, combine flour, salt, cayenne pepper and garlic powder. Shake to mix well. Trim fat from chicken, cut into 1-inch pieces then add to the bag. Shake to coat with flour and spices.

2. Heat oil in pressure cooker on medium-high heat and stir fry chicken in batches for about 3–5 minutes or until browned. Remove chicken and keep warm. Reserve the leftover seasoned flour.

3. Reduce to medium heat. Add celery and bell peppers then sauté for 3 minutes. Add onion and sauté until soft. add garlic and jalapeño pepper; sauté for 30 seconds.

4. Add beer, Worcestershire sauce, tomato sauce, chicken broth, marjoram and bay leaf. Close and lock the lid and bring to low pressure then maintain pressure for 20 minutes. Quick-release the pressure then remove the lid. Remove the bay leaf and discard.

5. Meanwhile, heat lard or bacon fat in a cast-iron skillet on medium heat. Add some water to the reserved seasoned flour and whisk to make a paste. Add flour paste to the skillet then cook with constant stirring for about 8-10 minutes or until the roux turns brown.

6. Whisk some of the juices in the pressure cooker into the roux in the cast iron skillet to loosen the mixture. Next, stir the roux into the stew in the pressure cooker.

7. Bring the stew to a simmer and cook for 3 minutes or until thick enough. Taste for seasoning and add additional salt or Worcestershire sauce, if needed, as well as black pepper to taste. Serve.

Barley, Chickpea And Cannellini Stew

With a light and delicate taste, some might find this stew too simple. But it is this simplicity that makes this dish a hit.

Preparation Time: 10 minutes

Cooking Time: 20 minutes

Number of Servings: 6

Ingredients:

3 coriander seeds

1 whole clove

4 cups water

2 tablespoons vegetable oil

1 heaping cup dried cannellini beans

1 heaping cup dried chickpeas, soaked

1/2 cup pearled barley

1 teaspoon white pepper

1 clove garlic

1 teaspoon salt

1 tablespoon extra-virgin olive oil

1/4 cup grated pecorino Romano cheese

Directions:

1. Combine the coriander seeds and clove in a bouquet garni or tea ball and place in pressure cooker. Add water, oil, beans, chickpeas, barley, white pepper and garlic to the pressure cooker. Close the lid and lock.

2. Turn up to high heat and when the cooker gets to pressure, lower to the minimum heat required maintain pressure. Cook for 15 minutes.

3. Open with the natural-release method—disengage the "keep warm" mode or unplug the cooker then open when the pressure indicator has gone down (20–30 minutes).

4. Season with salt to taste then top each serving with cheese and a swirl of olive oil.

Easy Vegetarian Stew
Try serving this vegan treat once in a while.

Preparation Time: 15 minutes

Cooking Time: 32 minutes

Number of Servings: 4

Ingredients:

2 tablespoons olive oil

2 stalks celery, sliced

1 bell pepper, diced

1 onion, chopped

1 28-ounce can crushed tomatoes

1 16-ounce package vegan chicken

2 cups uncooked corn kernels

1/2 cup barbecue sauce

1 cup ketchup

1 tablespoon vegan Worcestershire sauce

1 tablespoon liquid smoke

1 teaspoon salt

1/2 teaspoon black pepper

Directions:

1. Add olive oil to the pressure cooker and heat on medium heat. Sauté the celery, bell pepper and onion for about 5 minutes or until soft. Add the vegan chicken then cook until done according to the package directions.

2. Add the remaining ingredients. Close the lid and lock it; bring to high pressure then maintain for 30 minutes. Remove from heat and let the pressure release naturally.

Hearty Eggplant Stew
Healthy and nutritious, that's what this stew is all about.

Preparation Time: 15 minutes

Cooking Time: 32 minutes

Number of Servings: 4

Ingredients:

2 medium eggplants, cut into large cubes

1 russet potato, diced

1 14-ounce can chickpeas, drained

6 cups vegetable stock

1 cup tomatoes, diced

1 tablespoon tomato paste

1 tablespoon lemon juice

1 bay leaf

1 teaspoon cumin

1/2 cup parsley, chopped

2 teaspoons salt

Directions:

1. In the pressure cooker, combine all the ingredients. Close the lid and lock it.

2. Bring to low pressure and then maintain for 30 minutes. Remove from heat and let the pressure release naturally.

3. Remove bay leaf and adjust the seasoning before serving, if needed.

Turkey & Sausage Stew

This stew provides energy and nutrients needed for a healthy body.

Preparation Time: 15 minutes

Cooking Time: 32 minutes

Number of Servings: 4

Ingredients:

1 pound turkey breast, boneless, skinless, cut into bite-size pieces

1/2 pound smoked andouille sausage or kielbasa

2 tablespoons olive or vegetable oil

1 large sweet onion, peeled and diced

11/2 teaspoons dried thyme

4 cloves garlic, peeled and minced

1/2 teaspoon freshly ground black pepper

1/4 teaspoon dried red pepper flakes

1 teaspoon filé powder

1/4 teaspoon dried sage

1 14-ounce can chicken broth

1/2 cup white wine

2 stalks celery, sliced

3 bay leaves

1 10-ounce package frozen sliced okra, thawed

1 large green bell pepper, seeded and diced

1 15-ounce can diced tomatoes

1/2 cup fresh cilantro, minced

Directions:

1. Add oil to the pressure cooker and heat on medium heat. Add the turkey pieces, sausage slices and onion. Stir-fry for about 5 minutes or until turkey begins to brown and the onions are translucent.

2. Stir in thyme, garlic, black pepper, red pepper flakes, filé powder and sage.

3. Sauté for 1 minute and then pour in the wine to deglaze the pan, scraping the bottom of the pressure cooker so as to loosen anything stuck to the bottom. Stir in the remaining ingredients.

4. Close the lid, lock it and bring to low pressure. Maintain the pressure for 8 minutes. Remove from the heat and let the pressure release naturally.

5. Remove the lid. Remove bay leaves and discard. Taste for seasoning and add more if necessary.

Barley And Chickpeas Stew

Let's try this vegan treat, filling and good for the body.

Preparation Time: 10 minutes

Cooking Time: 15 minutes

Number of Servings: 4

Ingredients:

1 cup dry chickpeas, soaked

1 cup pearled barley

1 clove garlic, crushed

2 tablespoons olive oil, divided

2 carrots, diced

2 celery stalks, diced

1 large white onion, diced

4 cups water

2 teaspoons salt

1 teaspoon white pepper

Directions:

1. In the pressure cooker, combine all of the ingredients, except for the salt, pepper, and 1 tablespoon of olive oil.

2. Close the lid and lock. Turn up to high heat and when pressure is attained, lower to the minimum heat required to maintain pressure. Cook at high pressure for 15 minutes.

3. Open with the natural release method.

4. Stir in salt and pepper. Serve with a swirl of the reserved olive oil.

Asian Tofu Stew

Tofu as a substitute to meat comes into spotlight in this tasty stew.

Preparation Time: 5 minutes

Cooking Time: 9 minutes

Number of Servings: 2-4

Ingredients:

1 tablespoon sesame oil

1/2 onion, sliced

1 teaspoon fresh ginger, minced

1 clove garlic, minced

1 12.3-ounce package soft silken tofu, drained and cubed

1 cup shiitake mushrooms, sliced

1 cup shredded green cabbage

1 tablespoon crushed red pepper

1 teaspoon rice wine vinegar

1 teaspoon soy sauce

3 cups vegetable stock

3 piece kombu (seaweed)

2 green onions, sliced

Directions:

1. In the pressure cooker, heat sesame oil on medium heat then sauté onion for 3 minutes. Add ginger and garlic and sauté 30 seconds more.

2. Add tofu, mushrooms, cabbage, red pepper, vinegar, soy sauce, stock and kombu to the pressure cooker. Close the lid, lock it and bring to low pressure. Maintain pressure for 5 minutes. Remove from heat and let the pressure release naturally.

3. Remove the lid. Remove and discard the kombu then stir in green onions before serving.

Onion-Celery-Bell Stew

Preparation Time: 15 minutes

Cooking Time: 20 minutes

Number of Servings: 6

Ingredients:

10 tablespoons margarine or butter

1 cup green bell pepper, finely diced

1 cup celery, finely diced

1 cup white onion, finely diced

1 clove garlic, minced

2 tablespoons flour

2 cups water

2 ounces tomato paste

2 teaspoons salt

1 teaspoon black pepper

1/2 cup green onion, finely diced

1 tablespoon vegan Worcestershire sauce

1/2 teaspoon cayenne pepper

1/4 cup parsley, chopped

1 bay leaf

6 cups cooked white rice

Directions:

1. Add margarine or butter to pressure cooker and melt on medium-low heat. Add bell pepper, celery and onion; sauté for 4-5 minutes with frequent stirring. Add garlic and sauté for 1 minute more.

2. Stir in the flour to create a roux and cook for about 5 minutes.

3. Add the remaining ingredients except the rice. Close and lock the lid. Bring to medium pressure and maintain for 10 minutes. Remove from heat and let the pressure release naturally.

4. Remove bay leaf and discard. Serve over cooked white rice.

Veggie Combo Gumbo

The taste of this vegetable and chicken combo dish is unique. Try it!

Preparation Time: 15 minutes

Cooking Time: 32 minutes

Number of Servings: 6

Ingredients:

1/2 cup flour

1/2 cup vegetable oil

1 white onion, diced

2 stalks celery, diced

1 bell pepper, diced

2 cups vegetable stock

4 cloves garlic, minced

1 tablespoon vegan Worcestershire sauce

1 16-ounce package frozen chopped okra

1/2 teaspoon filé powder

1 bay leaf

1/2 cup flat-leaf parsley, chopped

1 pound vegan chicken, chopped

1/2 cup scallions, sliced

6 cups cooked white rice

4 cups water

2 teaspoons black pepper

1 tablespoon Cajun seasoning

2 teaspoons salt

Directions:

1. In the pressure cooker, bring oil and flour to medium heat. Stir and keep stirring for about 25 minutes until the roux attains a rich brown color.

2. Add the bell pepper, onion, garlic and celery to the roux and sauté 5 minutes. Add the water and then bring to a boil for 20 minutes over high heat.

3. Add the stock, vegan Worcestershire sauce, bay leaf, okra, Cajun seasoning, salt & pepper. Lock the lid and bring to low pressure and maintain that pressure for 1 hour. Let the pressure release naturally.

4. Add the rest of the ingredients except the rice, cook for 10 minutes over low heat.

5. Remove the bay leaf and then serve over cooked white rice.

Mushroom Stew With Oysters

The combination of mushroom and oyster flavors makes this stew irresistible.

Preparation Time: 15 minutes

Cooking Time: 32 minutes

Number of Servings: 6

Ingredients:

1/2 cup onions, diced

2 tablespoons butter

1/2 cup celery, diced

1/2 cup béchamel sauce

1 clove garlic, minced

1/2 teaspoon dried thyme

1 pound oyster mushrooms, chopped

2 cups heavy cream, or unsweetened soymilk

1/2 cup white wine

1 teaspoon lemon juice

Optional: Chopped parsley

1 teaspoon salt

Directions:

1. In the pressure cooker, heat the butter over medium heat. Now, add the onions and celery, sautéing for 5 minutes. Add the garlic and sauté again for another 30 seconds.

2. Add the mushrooms, béchamel sauce, white wine, thyme, cream and salt. Lock lid into place; bringing to low pressure and maintaining for 30 minutes. Remove and allow pressure release naturally.

3. Once released, remove the lid. If it isn't thick enough, bring back to the burner and simmer with the lid off over low heat. Add the lemon juice and stir.

4. If desired, stir in chopped parsley and serve.

Fish & Vegetable Stew
This dish is delicious. You will love it!

Preparation Time: 15 minutes

Cooking Time: 32 minutes

Number of Servings: 4

Ingredients:

1 large onion, peeled and diced

2 tablespoons butter

2 stalks celery, diced

4 medium potatoes, peeled &cut into 1/2-inch cubes

4 large carrots, peeled and diced

1 pound white fish fillets, firm-fleshed & cut into 1/2-inch pieces

1 cup cold water

2 cups fish stock or clam juice

1 bay leaf

1 cup heavy cream or milk

1/2 teaspoon dried thyme

1 cup thawed frozen or fresh corn kernels

Salt & freshly ground black or white pepper, to taste

Directions:

1. Add butter to pressure cooker, set on medium heat and bring to temperature. Add the onions; sauté until soft for about 3 minutes.

2. Add the celery, potatoes and carrot. Stir and sauté for 1 minute more. Add the fish, clam juice or fish stock, water, thyme and bay leaf.

3. Lock lid and bring pressure cooker to high pressure; maintain this pressure for 4 minutes. Release the pressure quickly.

4. Remove lid, tilting away from you so that any excess steam can escape easily.

5. Remove bay leaf and discard. Stir in the milk or cream and corn. Taste for seasoning and adjust accordingly with salt and pepper.

6. Simmer until chowder is hot and corn is cooked. Transfer to bowls and serve.

Stewy Chicken Super

Enjoy this great chicken stew with your family and friends.

Preparation Time: 10 minutes

Cooking Time: 50 minutes

Number of Servings: 8

Ingredients:

8 chicken thighs

3 tablespoons bacon fat

1/2 cup chicken broth or dry white wine

1 28-ounce can diced tomatoes

1/4 teaspoon sugar

2 large yellow onions, peeled &sliced

1 10-ounce package frozen and thawed whole kernel corn

1 10-ounce package of frozen okra, thawed & sliced

1 10-ounce package frozen & thawed lima beans

1 cup of bread crumbs, toasted

To taste: Salt & freshly ground black pepper

3 tablespoons Worcestershire sauce

2 cups water

Directions:

1. In the pressure cooker, bring the bacon fat to temperature over medium heat. Next, add 4 chicken thighs with their skin-sides down and fry until they are lightly browned.

2. Remove the fried thighs. Add the remaining thighs and fry. Return the initial 4 fried thighs to the pressure cooker. To it, add the water, onions, tomatoes, sugar and chicken broth or wine.

3. Lock the lid securely and bring to high pressure for 12 minutes. Quick-release pressure and remove lid. Remove the chicken and leave to cool.

4. Once cool, remove meat from the chicken bones and then discard the skin & bones. Shred chicken meat and set aside.

5. Add the corn, okra and lima beans to the pot. Bring to a simmer, cooking uncovered for about 30 minutes.

6. Add the shredded chicken, Worcestershire sauce and bread crumbs; stir and let it simmer for 10 minutes, stirring from time to time to thicken the stew.

7. Taste for seasoning. Add salt and pepper if necessary and hot sauce if needed.

Quick 'N' Easy Beef Stew

The recipe name says it all: A hearty stew that is so quick and easy to prepare.

Preparation Time: 15 minutes

Cooking Time: 10 minutes

Number of Servings: 8

Ingredients:

2 cups cooked roast beef, cut into pieces

1 10-ounce box frozen mixed vegetables

1 101/2-ounce can condensed French onion soup

1 24-ounce bag frozen vegetables for stew

1 103/4-ounce can condensed tomato soup

1 tablespoon Worcestershire sauce

1 tablespoon all-purpose flour

1 tablespoon butter

Salt & freshly ground black pepper to taste

2 cups water

Directions:

1. Add the soups, roast beef, frozen vegetables Worcestershire sauce and water to the pressure cooker.

2. Lock lid and bring to low pressure for 3 minutes. Remove from heat, release the pressure quickly and remove the lid.

3. Make a paste by mixing the butter into the flour to in a small bowl. Ladle 1/2 cup of the soup broth into this bowl and whisk into the paste. Pour into the stew.

4. Place pressure cooker, uncovered over medium-high heat and bring stew to a boil; boil 2 minutes, stirring from time to time.

5. Reduce the heat, simmer another 2 minutes or until the stew becomes thickened. Taste stew for seasoning, and if needed, add salt and pepper.

Tex-Mex Stew
Enjoy the taste of two worlds in this Mexico and Texas stew combo.

Preparation Time: 15 minutes

Cooking Time: 32 minutes

Number of Servings: 8

Ingredients:

2 tablespoons olive or vegetable oil

1 3 1/2-pound English or chuck roast, trim & cut into 1-inch cubes

1 7-ounce can green chilies

1 8-ounce can tomato sauce

2 15-ounce cans diced tomatoes

1 green bell pepper, seeded & diced

1 large sweet onion, peeled & diced

1 tablespoon ground cumin

6 cloves garlic, peeled and minced

1 teaspoon freshly ground black pepper

2 tablespoons lime juice

Cayenne pepper, to taste

2 jalapeño peppers, seeded & diced

1 bunch fresh cilantro, chopped

Directions:

1. Add oil to pressure cooker, bringing to temperature over medium-high heat.

2. Add the beef, stir-fry until thoroughly browned. Stir in the tomatoes, chilies, tomato sauce, bell pepper, onion, cumin, garlic, jalapeño peppers, cayenne ,black pepper and lime juice.

3. If necessary, add enough water or beef broth to cover the ingredients in the pressure cooker, but do not fill more than two-thirds full.

4. Lock lid securely and bring to low pressure for 1 hour. Remove from heat. Allow pressure to release of its own accord. Remove the lid, add the cilantro and stir in. Serve immediately.

20-Minute Quick Beef Stew

Preparation Time: 10 minutes

Cooking Time: 25 minutes

Number of Servings: 8

Ingredients:

3 pounds boneless stewing beef, cut into bite sized pieces

3 Tbs. olive oil

1/3 cup of all-purpose flour

1 large yellow onion, chopped finely

2 garlic cloves, crushed

1 1/2 cups red wine

2 carrots, peeled and cut into 1/2-inch pieces

2 celery stalks, cut into 1/2-inch pieces

1/2 lb. new potatoes, cut into 1/2-inch pieces

1 Tbs. tomato paste

1 1/2 cups of beef stock

3 fresh thyme sprigs

Salt and freshly ground pepper, to taste

Directions:

1. In a large bowl, place the flour and season. Mix in the beef to cover the seasoned flour. Set cooker to brown and add the olive oil.

2. Next, add the beef in two batches until golden. Take beef out and then set aside. Pour the wine in. Swill around, once simmering, to loosen stuck meat on the base

3. Put back the beef with the garlic, onions, celery, potatoes, carrots, stock, thyme and tomato paste.

4. Mix thoroughly, cover, bring to pressure and cook for 20mins. Cool, remove the lid. Place in a bowl.

Sweet-Sugared Beef Stew

The addition of sugar to this well- loved beef stew gives it an entirely new and refreshing taste.

Preparation Time: 15 minutes

Cooking Time: 32 minutes

Number of Servings: 6

Ingredients:

2 cloves garlic, minced

1 lb. stewing beef

1 large onion, minced

2 tablespoons canola oil

5 medium carrots, ½inch pieces

1 large potato, ½ inch cubed

1 large parsnip, 1 inch pieces

2 cups frozen peas 1 sweet potato, 1 inch pieces

1/2 cup tomato sauce

2 bay leaves

1/2 cup dry red or white wine

1 teaspoon Worcestershire sauce

1 teaspoon dried thyme

Salt and pepper to taste

1/2 cup water

Directions:

1. Heat the pressure cooker, add the oil and then fry the garlic and onions until clear.

2. Place meat in and fry until golden all over, stirring to prevent it from sticking. Add more oil if needed.

3. Add the remaining ingredients, mixing well. Secure lid and bring to pressure, cooking for the recommended time.

4. Cool and remove the lid. Stir and stir in frozen peas in. let it rest for awhile and then serve.

END OF THE BOX SET

Thank you for reading my book. If you enjoyed it, won't you please take a moment to leave me a good review at your retailer?

Thanks!

Rosa Barnes